Saint Peter's University Library
Jersey City, New Jersey 07306

Leonardo da Vinci

A STUDY IN PSYCHOSEXUALITY

Leonardo da Vinci

A STUDY IN PSYCHOSEXUALITY

by Sigmund Freud

AUTHORIZED TRANSLATION

by A. A. Brill, Ph.B., M.D.

VINTAGE BOOKS
A DIVISION OF RANDOM HOUSE
New York

VINTAGE BOOKS
are published by ALFRED A. KNOPF, INC.
and RANDOM HOUSE, INC.

Copyright, 1947, by A. A. Brill. All rights reserved under
International and Pan-American Copyright Conventions.

Library of Congress Catalog Card Number: 55-8302

Manufactured in the United States of America

Contents

Introduction by A. A. Brill **vii**

Leonardo da Vinci **3**

ILLUSTRATIONS
facing pages indicated

Leonardo da Vinci 58

Mona Lisa 59

The Holy Family 90

John the Baptist 91

Introduction

BY A. A. BRILL, PH.B., M.D.

In the minds of most people, even among the intelligentsia, Freud is still closely associated with sex. To be sure, he threw much light on this primary instinct, yet this is only a very small part of his great achievements. This association, this linking of sex and Freud, as if they had appeared in the same breath, is based on the fact that, after sex had been kept more or less incarcerated for almost two thousand years in the nether regions of civilized mankind, Freud discovered it, as it were, and established that it was not only astir, but often very meddlesome. But as it had not been permitted to function openly and naturally since the passing of Pagan culture, sex went

Introduction

underground and behaved like an outcast who, plying his trade secretly and sneakily, often causes confusion by popping up where and when least expected.

However, when one looks back to the two generations that followed Freud's dictum that *no neurosis is possible in a normal sexual life,* one is amazed at the changes that have occurred since then in our whole mode of living. The riddle of the neuroses which had baffled mankind from the beginning of civilization had been solved as soon as Freud demonstrated that the neuroses were direct descendants of the despised Eros. The same happened to folklore, fairy tales and myths, which, like dreams, are now capable of solution. Indeed, all mental disciplines have thus been almost entirely rewritten since psychoanalysis came on the scene. But lest I be carried away by paeans to the great master, I must restrict myself to that part of Freud's discoveries which is still closely associated with his name, namely, sex.

There were many other scientists, daring thinkers, who wrote and speculated about the instinct of sex and its manifestations, even before Freud. We have in mind Havelock Ellis, v. Krafft-Ebing, Paolo Mantegazza, Magnus Hirsch-

Introduction

feld, Iwan Bloch and many others. They all left very valuable contributions, which laid the foundation for a scientific understanding of sex, but it remained for Freud to correlate all these findings with those he discovered psychoanalytically and thus give us a full understanding of normal and abnormal sexuality. For the writers who preceded Freud centered most of their investigations on sexual manifestations of adults, and to some extent on deviations from the normal. Hence what they described was usually regarded as something alien to the normal person. Indeed, up to the advent of Freud, the average person would only reluctantly admit that he had anything to do with sex, nor could he imagine that sex had any direct relation to children. If anything occasionally cropped up in scientific or lay publications concerning sex in children, it was quickly rejected as something inapplicable to innocent youngsters.

This neglect or side-stepping of sex in the face of great advances in other human problems was largely due to the fact that sex, which the Pagan world considered natural, was systematically suppressed by the new followers of the Messiah. The Greeks and Romans exalted beauty and even deified sex, but St. Paul, the ascetic apostle said

Introduction

in his First Epistle to the Corinthians: "It is good for a man not to touch a woman. . . ." "But if they cannot contain let them marry; for it is better to marry than to burn." The early Church fathers not only made every effort to follow the Jewish austere views of sexuality, but, as is always the case in new movements, they surpassed them in rigidity. For the Jews were quite sensible about sex. They were, to be sure, against sex worship and everything that went with it, but they allowed sufficient play for Eros to insure healthy sex living. But the Church fathers lost all sense of proportion in their zeal to exterminate the erotic from their followers. Beauty, the ruling passion of the Greeks, soon gave way to ugliness, and cleanliness which was later put next to godliness, had no place in saintliness. On the contrary, "The purity of the body and its garments," said St. Paul, "means the impurity of the soul." [1]

Following the Dark Ages the Renaissance strove hard to revive the wisdom and splendor that was ancient Greece and Rome. Bold spirits began to undig the now-mutilated Venuses, and to record the forgotten thoughts of the Ionian

[1] Havelock Ellis; *Studies in the Psychology of Sex*, Vol. IV, p. 31. Random House, New York.

Introduction

sages; slowly but surely the European world returned to sanity. Yet, despite continual progress in art and literature, sex, to which they were deeply indebted, was kept in the background. The science of medicine, which progressively developed new methods of medical and surgical treatment even for venereal diseases, kept discreetly silent about the normal manifestations of sex. Even when it was no longer a sin to indulge in legitimate sex, few if any scientists studied the normal sex functions in the same manner as those of the heart or stomach. This attitude continued into our own times, and when Freud made the provocative statement that all neurotic symptoms are traceable to sexual disturbances, his colleagues were impressively shocked. Since 1893, the new theories of Breuer and Freud[2] on hysteria were hailed as stimulating and fruitful discoveries, but as Freud continued to stress the sexual factor in the neuroses he was, so to speak, excommunicated by the medical world. Breuer, his collaborator and friend, made some effort to defend him, but as the storm kept on increasing he, too, withdrew from the psychoanalytic scene. Freud, himself,

[2] *Studies in Hysteria,* transl. by A. A. Brill, Monograph Series of Nervous and Mental Diseases.

Introduction

was surprised at this vehement reaction; as an experienced researcher and close observer, he could not quite understand this sudden outburst. In his *History of the Psychoanalytic Movement*[3] Freud relates that he really did not deserve the credit for the injection of sexual concepts into the genesis of the neuroses. He heard this view from two of his former teachers, Charcot and Chroback, who independently observed that sex played a part in the etiology of the neuroses. Their remarks, casually expressed, lay dormant in his mind for a long time; he gave no thought to them for years, but as he continued to analyze his patients' mental productions they grew in intensity and took on definite form. The more analytic material he obtained, the more convinced he became of the ubiquity of sex in the etiology of the neuroses.

When I presented Freud's theories in New York City I had the same experience that he had in Vienna. Despite the repeated forewarnings which he had given me, I still wondered why psychiatrists and neurologists, my most implacable opponents, were so deeply shocked by Freud's theories of sex in the neuroses. I could

[3] *The Basic Writings of Sigmund Freud*, p. 933, transl. by A. A. Brill, Modern Library, 1938.

Introduction

not quite grasp why these scholarly gentlemen, most of them authorities in their respective fields, did not possess enough objectivity to see that sex did play an important role in everybody's life, and especially in the lives of those sensitive individuals designated as neurotics. Their seeming blindness to the role of sex in normal and neurotic life was a great surprise to me because I was well aware that physicians, particularly psychiatrists, have always attached importance to the role of sex in nervous and mental diseases. I recalled that long before I ever heard of Freud, in my pre-medical life, most young people thought that masturbation made one nervous, that it was likely to produce insanity and other dreadful maladies, and that *fellatio,* called by another name, was responsible for "softening of the brain." Later, as a medical student, our professor of neurology taught us that sex played a great part in the etiology of both organic and functional nervous diseases. Professor M. Allan Starr, in his lectures and in his book, repeated that sexual excesses played a part in the etiology of tabes, Friedrichs ataxia, myelitis, and neurasthenia. Yet only six or seven years later when I read a paper on Freud's theories of the neuroses in the New York Acad-

Introduction

emy of Medicine, Professor Starr vented violent opposition to Freud because he injected sex into the etiology of the neuroses.

In order to clarify this puzzling problem to myself I decided to examine the psychiatric literature of the pre-Freudian times. I wished to know what the older psychiatrists and neurologists of the last, and of the early part of this, century thought about the role of sex in the neuroses. From the large amount of material perused, I selected the following characteristic views: W. Griesinger[4] states: *"Sexual excesses have a similar double injurious influence, in consequence of the mental excitement which is frequently associated therewith, and owing to the psychical exhaustion which results. The same may be said of onanism, which is likewise an important and frequent cause of insanity. Besides the emission of semen, and the direct action of the often permanent irritation of the genital organ on the spinal cord and the brain, onanism certainly has a still more injurious action on the mental state and a more direct influence on the production of insanity."* He quotes authorities

[4] *Mental Pathology and Therapeutics*, p. 173, transl. by Robertson & Rutherford, London 1867.

Introduction

who ascribe the majority of all the cases treated in public asylums as due to onanism.

This statement plainly shows that Griesinger had pronounced views on the importance of sex in nervous and mental diseases. Like all the other psychiatrists and neurologists, not only of his time but also those who preceded and followed him, Griesinger attributed many mental ailments to sexual excesses and masturbation.

William H. Hammond[5] states that excessive venereal indulgence and masturbation are causes of insanity. His son, Graeme Hammond, followed in his father's footsteps. He too believed that sexual excesses or sexual transgressions must play a subsidiary part in the causation of tabes, in chronic myelitis, and even in progressive muscular dystrophy.

J. C. Bucknill, and Daniel Hack Tuke,[6] though doubting that the sexual vice is a cause of insanity, nevertheless quote the following outstanding authorities to confirm this view: Esquirol stated that 5 per cent of the female admissions to the Salpetrière were attributed to prostitutes; Dr. Earl claimed that nineteen out of 572

[5] *A Treatise of Diseases of the Nervous System,* p. 377.
[6] *Manual of Psychological Medicine,* 1874.

Introduction

male admissions to the Northampton State Lunatic Hospital (Massachusetts) were attributed to masturbation; Drs. Bell and Ray of the McLean Asylum (Massachusetts) described cases (p. 343) of a form of moral insanity due to masturbation, and Schroeder Van der Kolk, who, describing (p. 345) such forms of insanity, stated: "If one perceives in a young man a certain shyness, and an evasion and castdown look, and a dull irresolute character, which are soon accompanied by stupidity and confusion of head, and weakness of memory, then one must be mindful of this sad vice."

Dr. Charles H. Handfield [7] quotes Dr. Copeland to the effect that "increased reflex excitability of the nerves of the female generative organs is one of the principal causative conditions of hysterical effects, and that an erethism proceeding from the generative apparatus might, I can well conceive, give rise to erotomania."

From the quotations just cited it can be readily seen that these authors knew very little, if anything, about sex and its functions. Their statements, as everybody now knows, were not based on scientific facts, but followed a cliché which had existed for centuries. Kraepelin, the

[7] *Clinical Observations on Functional Nervous Diseases.*

Introduction

father of modern psychiatry, clearly showed toward the end of the last century that masturbation, frequently observed in psychotics of both sexes, is the effect rather than the cause of the disease. For masturbation is practically a universal phenomenon in normal life, and has long been considered by sexologists as a part of the normal evolution of modern sex life.

However, as time went on, the perniciousness of sex in nervous and mental diseases, though doubted, was by no means entirely abandoned. Thus Dr. Jerome K. Bandy, Professor of Psychological Medicine and Diseases of the Nervous System,[8] states: "It has often been said that hysteria is generally developed in spinsters, widows, or women who live separated from their husbands and that it is an unrelieved erethysm of the sexual organs that produces the hysterical manifestations. This view has caused many older writers to advise marriage as a means of curing hysteria in single women. But I am far from concurring in this opinion, considering it an injustice to many pure and noble women to misjudge them in this respect simply because they are hysterical." Dr. Bandy goes on to say that hysteria is found in prostitutes whose erotic

[8] *Lectures on Diseases of the Nervous System*, p. 292, 1876.

Introduction

faculties are sufficiently developed and satisfied, and that many husbands told him that far from being sexually very excitable, their hysterical wives are disagreeably cold and indifferent, which shows that passion has nothing to do with the disease.

Despite Dr. Bandy's admonition that marriage is not a cure-all for hysteria, I have seen many women who were married against their will in order to cure them of a nervous or mental disease. Moreover, although Dr. Bandy absolved unrequited sex from any responsibility for the production of hysteria in spinsters, widows and single women, he nevertheless considers it an injustice to think that "pure and noble women" are in any way affected by sex. Dr. Bandy seemed to have sensed something which he did not quite understand, because he did not know anything about the nature of sex.

Dr. Henry Maudsley, whose works of three generations ago can be read with interest and profit by modern psychiatrists, states: "The development of the sexual system at puberty and the great revolution which is thereby affected in mental life must needs often give a color to the phenomena of insanity occurring after

Introduction

puberty."[9] Dr. Maudsley then cites cases of insanity in both sexes as due to masturbation.

After I had perused the numerous books from which I have quoted, I wondered what the "Patron Saint" of American psychiatry had to say on the subject. For my opponents were all members of the American Psychiatric Association, whose flag is adorned with the portrait of Benjamin Rush, who was not only a great psychiatrist but a great American, one of the signers of the Declaration of Independence. In his *Medical Inquiries and Observations upon the Diseases of the Mind*[10] he had this to say on sex and mental diseases: "This appetite which was implanted in our natures for the purpose of propagating the species, when excessive, becomes a disease both of the body and mind. When restrained, it produces tremors, a flushing of the face, sighing, nocturnal pollutions, hysteria, hypochondriasis, and in women the *furor uterinus*." He then goes on to say that sexual excesses and onanism produce impotence, dysuria, tabes dorsalis, "pulmonary consumption," dyspepsia,

[9] Maudsley: *The Physiology and Pathology of the Mind*, p. 251. Appleton & Co. New York, 1867.
[10] Philadelphia, 1827.

Introduction

dimness of sight, vertigo, epilepsy, hypochondriasis, loss of memory, manolgia, fatuity and death" (p. 345). Dr. Rush then cites cases to illustrate his views. Dr. Rush was no prude; his discussions of problems of sexual maladjustment could be read with profit by modern physicians, and as shown by the above quotation he had no doubt about the role of sex in mental diseases, though like others who lived before the newer discoveries, he attributed too much power to excessive sexuality and masturbation.

At the beginning of the twentieth century, we find that v. Krafft-Ebing, the author of the widely read *Psychopathia Sexualis,* states in his *Textbook on Insanity:*[11] "The significance of abuse of the sexual organs in the origin of neuropsychoses and psychoses is by no means small. . . . Sexual excesses may create a predisposition to mental diseases, intensify a predisposition already present, or act as an accessory cause. The intermediate factor in the pathogenesis of nervous and mental diseases in neurasthenia is induced by *abusus veneris.*" Dr. v. Krafft-Ebing fully describes a "masturbation insanity," and as far as I can ascertain, he originated the entity *Erotic Paranoia* (Erotomania), concerning which

[11] Transl. by Chaddock, p. 185-6, 1904.

Introduction

he states: "The nucleus of the whole malady is the delusion of being distinguished and loved by a person of the opposite sex who regularly belongs to the higher classes of society. The love for this person is, as should be emphasized, romantic, enthusiastic, but absolutely platonic. Such individuals fall in love with a lady, usually older than themselves, whom they have never seen, or whom they have only rarely seen."

Dr. v. Krafft-Ebing, as is well known, was very interested in sex. Throughout his works he strove to evaluate the sexual factors in the neuroses and psychoses. His contributions to the aberration of sex laid the foundation for a psychosexual pathology, yet he grievously erred about the role of masturbation in these maladies. Nor do we know what he really meant by sexual excesses or sexual abuse.

Weygand in his *Psychiatrie*[12] states that onanism is so widespread that it cannot be considered a sign of psychic abnormality, but it favors the development of neurasthenia. He also mentions the fact that the laity implicitly assumes that organic diseases of the spine and brain can be caused by sexual and generative processes.

[12] Lehmann's Verlag, München, 1902.

Introduction

Although Dr. Weygand no longer believed that masturbation is a sign of abnormal mentality, he still thought it favored neurasthenia, but he did not tell us how.

Leonardo Bianchi[13] fully accepts Freud's views of hysteria, but states that masturbation wastes and exhausts the brain (*per l'onanismo il cervello è piu logaro o stanco*), that melancholia in many youths is due to excessive onanism (p. 651), that one of the etiological factors of neurasthenia is sexual abuse, especially onanism (*gli abusi sessuali soppratutto poi l'onanismo*), and that *Confusione Mentale* (Mental Confusion), a form of psychosis found in predisposed young men, is due to uncontrollable onanism. Like Weygand, Bianchi belongs to this generation. He evidently gave considerable thought to Freud's theories, as can be readily seen from his textbook, but he is still more or less confused about the role of sex in nervous and mental diseases.

I could quote from many other works of the last, and the beginning of this, century which express similar views. I have not, however, delved deeply into the psychiatric work beyond the first decade of this century, but on acci-

[13] *Tratto di Psychiatria,* Napoli.

Introduction

dentally reading such an authoritative work as Church and Peterson,[14] I found that in their 1911 edition these authors still give masturbation and sexual excesses in "the general etiology of insanity."

In sum, the above quotations, selected at random from a great many authors, definitely show that the earlier as well as the later students of psychiatry have always associated sex with nervous and mental maladies. There is no doubt that they all felt that sex played a role in their patients' maladies, but as they knew little about the evolution of sex in normal and abnormal life, they did not know how to formulate their views. Their objection to Freud's theories of sex in the neuroses, as I see it, was based on the *universality of the sexual factors* which Freud claimed for the neuroses. As they have always attached degenerative stigma to hysteria and to other psychic diseases, they found it quite natural to associate them with masturbation, sexual excesses and abuses of sex, whatever that meant to them, but they waxed indignant when Freud removed the stigma of degeneracy from the neuroses and broadened the concept of sex to make

[14] Church and Peterson: *Nervous and Mental Diseases,* W. B. Saunders, Philadelphia, 1911.

Introduction

it applicable to normals, neurotics, and children. They were especially shocked at the idea that neurotic children, perhaps in their own family, should be associated with sex. They seemingly forgot that, while postulating sexuality in the neuroses, Freud at the same time broadened the concept of sex into the love-life of the individual. Sex no longer meant some physical expression relating to the genitals. That was only a small part of it, but it embraced everything that dealt with love in the broad sense of this term. For we must bear in mind that it was only a generation or so ago that intelligent people began to look upon sex with open eyes, without being shocked by the very word. Thus, in 1908, I sent my first analysis of a case of dementia praecox to *The Journal of Abnormal Psychology*. Dr. Morton Prince, the editor of the *Journal*, wrote me a very nice letter accepting the paper for publication.[15] In fact, he was quite enthusiastic about it. But he asked my permission to change one word which he evidently disliked. That word was "homosexual." I did not discuss homosexuality in this paper; I merely said that there may have been some

[15] "Psychological Factors in Dementia Praecox," *The Journal of Abnormal Psychology*, Vol. III, No. 4, 1909.

Introduction

homosexual relations between the patient and his landlady's son. As Dr. Prince was one of our outstanding psychopathologists, and my paper was to be published in *The Journal of Abnormal Psychology,* his request was really amazing. I gave him permission to change the word for any other word which would express the same meaning, but Dr. Prince evidently found no word "less obnoxious"; so he let it stand. I mention this incident to show the prevailing state of affairs about sex in this country in the beginning of this century.

In order to help those readers who are not fully conversant with Freud's views on sex, I will give here a brief resumé of some of his theories, especially of those that are pertinent to the sexual phenomena discussed in the present volume. After studying patients psychoanalytically for over ten years, Freud published a small but concise volume in which he gives his conception of the psychosexual development of man.[16] As I said before, Freud found it necessary to broaden the concept of sex to make it applicable not only to neurotics, but also to

[16] *Three Contributions to the Theory of Sex,* p. 553, *The Basic Writings of Sigmund Freud,* transl. by A. A. Brill, The Modern Library, New York, 1938.

Introduction

normal adults, to children, as well as to those phenomena which have hitherto been considered as something *sui generis,* as something alien to normal sexuality. In this book, now regarded as a classic, Freud begins his discussion by introducing the term *libido* which, in contradistinction to the meanings given to it by others, he defines as the motive force of the sexual life. In psychoanalysis, libido means a sum of energy usually directed to an outer object. This energy, though changeable, is not yet measurable, and comprises all impulses and components of love in the broad sense; it is thus a more comprehensive physical function striving for pleasure in general. Its principal component however is sexual love with sexual union as its aim, but it is not as closely connected with the genitals as was hitherto believed. As a matter of fact, libido only secondarily enters into the service of reproduction, for it functions actively also in self-love, love between parents and children, friendships, attachments to concrete objects, and in devotions to abstract ideas.

In the child the whole libido is centered in the ego and is termed *ego libido*. In the early time of development the child is purely egoistic; he needs nothing from the outer world to sus-

Introduction

tain him and keep him contented except his mother, whom the child does not consider as outside of himself. This state of affairs persists more or less during the first four years of life, but as the child grows older his ego libido gradually changes into *narcissistic libido*. This phase of development begins about the age of four and continues until about the age of six, during which period the libido, though still egoistic, gradually assumes an erotic tinge. Like Narcissus of the Greek myth, the child then loves himself above everything and everyone else, and actually obtains pleasure from himself.

Following the narcissistic phase, Freud speculatively postulated a *latency period,* which he phyletically compares to the glacial age, because during these years the child's sexuality is practically quiescent. This period from six to nine years may also be designated as the school age, for in civilized life the child is at that age usually sent to school, where, in contact with others, he learns how to give up some of his narcissism by giving and taking libido with outsiders and thus advance to a higher level of adjustment, to the stage of *object libido*.

This stage is well established at the age of puberty when in the normal course of events the

Introduction

individual attains what Freud calls *genitality* and *object finding*. Hitherto the child's outlets were sexual, but at puberty they become preponderantly genital. "Sexuality" thus connotes the whole process of development, while "genitality" represents its final stage. The child is, so to say, *polymorphous perverse* insofar as he seeks and obtains pleasure from so-called erogenous zones, i.e. from the mouth, the anus, the genitals, and the whole skin region, whereas all these stimuli in the adult lead directly to the genitals. Sexuality is thus widely disseminated, whereas genitality is directly channeled into one specific region. In other words, if everything proceeded normally, all the primary partial impulses and components of sex are by this time partially repressed, partially sublimated and the rest which retains its pure form is subjugated to the primacy of the genitals for the purpose of propagation. A certain amount of aggression, looking, showing off, touching, tasting and smelling then actively participate in the search for an object and in mating, and are normal concomitants of these processes.

In his effort to explain sexual aberrations Freud introduced two terms: *Sexual object* and *sexual aim,* which he uses to describe sexual behavior. The sexual object is the person from whom sexual attraction emanates, and the sexual aim represents the aim toward which the instinct strives. Normally the sexual object is a person of the opposite sex, and the sexual aim is the desire for normal coitus. As physicians have always learned normal processes by comparison with abnormal ones, Freud begins his three contributions to the theory of sex with a description of the sexual aberrations. He discusses, first, the deviations in reference to the sexual object and, second, those in reference to the sexual aim. The former group comprises among others a large class of people, estimated from one to three per cent of the male population, which are variously designated as inverts, homosexuals and by other names. The sexual object of these deviates is always a person of the same sex, while the opposite sex exerts no erotic appeal on them. On the contrary, persons of the opposite sex not only leave them cold, but often inspire them with repugnance. Many overt homosexuals speak of a *horror feminae* (a horror of women) which they claim to experience when confronted with the physical or erotic ele-

Introduction

ments of femininity. Many inverts do not, however, dislike women otherwise; on the contrary, they often prefer feminine companionship.

Moreover, we must bear in mind that homosexual acts, which not infrequently occur among young men or women in schools, in colleges, or wherever the sexes happen to be segregated for some time—that such sporadic homosexual relations do not constitute pathological or overt homosexuality. This form of homosexuality is diagnosed when there is a definite sensual need for a person of one's own sex accompanied by the same emotional feelings that are normally felt toward people of the opposite sex. In other words, the pronounced male invert experiences the same emotions for his sexual object as the love-stricken heterosexual for his love object.

However, the sexual instinct, like its analogous instinct of hunger, does not function in the same way in each and every person. As a matter of fact, it is impossible to give a definite estimate of the amount of food that each person requires in order to live and sustain himself in healthy comfort; that depends on many factors, on age, temperament and on constitutional make-up. This is even more true of the sexual instinct which manifests a more delicate and more com-

Introduction

plicated form of adjustment. There is no doubt, however, that every human being, like every animal, needs nourishment and craves sex. Society, taking note of this, exerts its greatest efforts to educate its members for proper adjustment to these two primary instincts. But, as we are here primarily interested in homosexual adjustment, we will add that, between the normal or heterosexual and the overt homosexual, there are many intermediary forms which, though ordinarily unrecognizable, nevertheless exist and now and then come to the notice of the psychiatrist.[17]

It was Freud's merit to have demonstrated that everything abnormal has its normal roots, and that no matter how well endowed an individual may be at birth, an accidental factor in childhood may change his whole course of life. This holds true in both normals and neurotics and is particularly demonstrable when we study the deviations in reference to the sexual object and sexual aim. Let us repeat that the normal sexual aim strives for a union of the genitals in the characteristic act of copulation. This act, which is analogous to the satisfaction

[17] Brill: *Lectures on Psychoanalytic Psychiatry*, Lect. IX, Knopf, New York, 1946.

Introduction

of hunger, reduces the sexual tension and temporarily quenches the sexual desire. However, a casual examination of even the most normal sexual act shows that any of the features which enter into its formation when exaggerated may lead to aberrations described as perversions. Thus any of the partial impulses which normally participate in the sexual act, such as aggression, touching or looking, may become magnified through some accidental infantile experience and later cause the individual to become a sadist or masochist,[18] toucheur or voyeur. But in both deviations there are also intermediate forms, ranging from normal to inversion or perversion. Thus there are men who are "show-offs," who strive to be in the limelight, while others shun everything that savors of sex; some are very aggressive in their various vocations, and life in general, while still others manifest the obverse of the picture and often give the impression of marked passivity. None of these types, however, are necessarily pathological. The most that we can say about them is that they show a certain up or down accentuation of these partial

---

[18] Brill: *Freud's Contribution to Psychiatry*, p. 88, W. W. Norton, New York, 1943.

Introduction

impulses and components which are normally common to every person.

The same may be said of the intermediates between inverts and normals. The old eccentric bachelor may be a devoted son who was unintentionally robbed of his masculinity by a loving mother. Or he may belong to that small class of males who are sexually below par,[19] or last, but not least, he may be one of those exceptional males who, though seemingly endowed with normal sexuality, have the capacity to sublimate it *in toto*. Such men have often been suspected of homosexuality, yet although different from the average, they cannot justifiably be designated as overt homosexuals. Ancient and modern literature furnishes many examples of deep love between men in which there was no tinge of sensuality. Thus the Bible tells of David and Jonathan, and from Plutarch we know of Damon and Pythias, each of whom was extremely devoted to the other. Thus David, lamenting the death of Jonathan, called him "brother" and said: "Thy love to me was wonderful, passing the love of women," and David, as all readers of the

[19] Brill: *Sex and the Physician, The Urologic and Cutaneous Review*, 1929.

Introduction

Bible know, was not at all unappreciative of the love and charms of women. The love of Damon and Pythias is proverbial for ideal friendship; no sensuality played any part in it. In the literature of our own times we often encounter similar examples. Thus Herman Melville, the author of *Moby Dick*, certainly felt great devotion to men, judging by his descriptions of his feelings for them. In his *Mardi* he speaks of an old seaman, one Jarl, whose "hands were brawny as the paws of a bear; his voice hoarse" and who was very illiterate, but "Now, higher sympathies apart, for Jarl I had a wonderful liking; for he loved me; from the first he had cleaved to me." Melville then tells how old mariners sometimes conceive a very strong attachment for some young sailor, his shipmate, "an attachment so devoted as to be wholly inexplicable, unless originating in that heart-loneliness which overtakes most seamen, as they grow aged, impelling them to fasten on some chance object of regard. But, however it was, my Viking, thy unbidden affection was the noblest homage ever paid me."

I selected these lines from one of Melville's works to illustrate the fact that between normal

Introduction

and abnormal there are many gradations. To my knowledge, Melville led a normal psychosexual existence; there was never any intimation that he was anything but sexually normal. Yet, judging by his attitude toward men, not only as expressed in this quotation but from many of his other works, notably from his idealization of Jack Chase, a fellow sailor to whom he dedicated his last work, one is justified in saying that Melville's normal homosexual component was more or less accentuated. Having endured the hardships of a sailor on a merchantman, whaler and man-of-war in the beginning of the last century, his mind must have often yearned for that period of his existence when he was in a nice home surrounded by the love and protection of parents, especially of a mother. During such stress one can easily empathize himself back into the early stage of life and gladly accept the love of an old sailor who would guide and protect him. Some might call his idealization of Jack Chase homosexual, in the sense that we all have a normal homosexual component which enables us to carry on philanthropic relations and friendships with our own sex. In other words, Melville's feelings represent a higher de-

Introduction

gree of homosexuality than one ordinarily encounters in daily life, but contains no taint of abnormality.

Melville was not the only litterateur who expressed such deep feelings for his own sex. Marlowe, Shakespeare, Montaigne, Tennyson, to mention only some, have expressed themselves so fervently about men that they have actually been accused of pathological homosexuality, yet nothing in their lives could justify such assumption. All we can repeat is that because of their artistic make-up, their normal homosexual component was more or less accentuated and, being what they were, they had the gift to express it more exuberantly. In none of these men has it ever been shown that they craved any sensual gratification from the men they revered. In their times, when the world was still under the spell of the old Church fathers, any fervent expression for a person of the same sex was immediately interpreted into something abnormal. Thanks to Freud we now know differently.

I was impelled to speak briefly about this (to some) delicate problem because Leonardo da Vinci was accused, tried and acquitted of homosexuality. There is no doubt that the accusations were based on some facts which were evidently

Introduction

misinterpreted. Da Vinci, Michelangelo and other great artistic geniuses were sensitive to the human form and certainly showed it in their artistic creations. As long as their expressions were directed to persons of the opposite sex, they were highly admired, but, when they dared evince the same feelings for their own sex, they were suspected and accused of homosexuality. In the light of our present knowledge, we have no right to express any definite opinion about psychic processes without knowing much more than we know about these great men. There is one thing, however, that obtrudes itself when we wonder whether Leonardo da Vinci was really an overt homosexual: he was a very truthful person, almost naïvely so. Nothing was found while he was living, nor in what he left in his works, to stamp him as an overt homosexual. Unconsciously, however, his life was influenced by many factors which in our times often produce this aberration. Freud ingeniously took these few fragments and gave us a most provocative portrait of this outstanding man, *ex ossicula Dinosauria*, as it were. From the infantile phantasy which Leonardo recalled while he was still in his cradle, Freud masterfully reconstructed the whole unconscious psychic life of the most

Introduction

inscrutable, the most fascinating personage of the Renaissance. Utilizing his psychoanalytic technique, Freud collected and sifted all available fragments from Leonardo's life and age, grouped them around Leonardo's vulture-phantasy and then combined all these single facts into one organic unity. The general principles which he discovered in this manner then fully explained Leonardo's incomprehensible traits of character.

But in working through this paleopsychological material, Freud not only gives us a profound insight into the psychosexual evolution of the child, but also shows how psychic experiences of childhood may lead to a neurosis, perversion or abnormality—an understanding of which is of the utmost value to every earnest student of normal and abnormal psychology.

February, 1947

Leonardo da Vinci

A STUDY IN PSYCHOSEXUALITY

One

When psychoanalytic investigation, which usually contents itself with frail human material, approaches the great personages of humanity, it is not impelled to it by motives which are often imputed to it by laymen. It does not strive "to blacken the radiant and to drag the sublime into the mire"; it finds no satisfaction in diminishing the distance between the perfection of the great and the inadequacy of the ordinary objects. But it cannot help finding that everything is worthy of understanding that can be perceived through those prototypes, and it also believes that none is so big as to be ashamed of being subject to the laws which control the

Leonardo da Vinci

normal and morbid actions with the same strictness.

Leonardo da Vinci (1452-1519) was admired even by his contemporaries as one of the greatest men of the Italian Renaissance; still, even then he appeared as mysterious to them as he now appears to us. An all-sided genius, "whose form can only be divined but never happily fathomed,"[1] he exerted the most decisive influence on his time as an artist; and it remained to us to recognize his greatness as a naturalist, which was united in him with the artist. Although he left masterpieces of the art of painting, while his scientific discoveries remained unpublished and unused, the investigator in him has never quite left the artist. Often it has severely injured the artist and in the end it has perhaps suppressed the artist altogether. According to Vasari, Leonardo reproached himself during the last hour of his life for having insulted God and men because he had not done his duty to his art.[2] And even if Vasari's story lacks all probability and belongs to those legends which began to be woven about the mystic master

[1] In the words of J. Burckhard, cited by Alexandra Konstantinowa, *Die Entwicklung des Madonnentypus bei Leonardo da Vinci*, Strassburg, 1907.
[2] *Vite*, etc. LXXXIII. 1550-1584.

A Study in Psychosexuality

while he was still living, it nevertheless retains indisputable value as a testimonial of the judgment of those people and of those times.

What was it that removed the personality of Leonardo from the understanding of his contemporaries? Certainly not the many-sidedness of his capacities and knowledge, which allowed him to install himself as a player of the lyre, on an instrument invented by himself, in the court of Lodovico Sforza, nicknamed Il Moro, the Duke of Milan, or which allowed him to write to the same person that remarkable letter in which he boasts of his abilities as a civil and military engineer. For the combination of manifold talents in the same person was not unusual in the time of the Renaissance; to be sure, Leonardo himself typified one of the most splendid examples of such persons. Nor did he belong to that type of genial persons who are outwardly poorly endowed by nature, and who in their own behalf place no value on the outer forms of life, and in the painful gloominess of their feelings fly from human relations. On the contrary, he was tall and symmetrically built, of consummate beauty of countenance and of unusual physical strength; he was charming in his manner, a master of speech, and jovial and affectionate to everybody. He loved beauty in the objects of his surroundings; he was fond of wearing magnificent garments and appreciated every refinement of conduct. In his treatise[3] on the art of painting he compares in a significant passage the art of painting with its sister arts and thus discusses the difficulties of the sculptor: "Now his face is entirely smeared and powdered with marble dust, so that he looks like a baker. He is covered with small marble splinters, so that it seems as if it snowed on his back, and his house is full of stone splinters, and dust. The case of the painter is quite different from that, for the painter is well dressed and sits with great comfort before his work; he gently and very lightly brushes in the beautiful colors. He wears as decorative clothes as he likes, and his house is filled with beautiful paintings and is spotlessly clean. He often enjoys company, music, or someone may read for him various nice works, and all this can be listened to with great pleasure, undisturbed by any pounding from the hammer and other noises."

It is quite possible that the conception of a beaming, jovial and happy Leonardo was true

[3] *Traktat von der Malerei,* new edition and introduction by Marie Herzfeld, E. Diederichs, Jena, 1909.

A Study in Psychosexuality

only for the first and longer period of the master's life. From now on, when the downfall of the rule of Lodovico Sforza forced him to leave Milan, his sphere of action and his assured position, to lead an unsteady and unsuccessful life until his last asylum in France, it is possible that the luster of his disposition became pale and some odd features of his character became more prominent. The turning of his interest from his art to science, which increased with age, must also have been responsible for widening the gap between himself and his contemporaries. All his efforts with which, according to their opinion, he wasted his time instead of diligently filling orders and becoming rich as perhaps his former classmate, Perugino, seemed to his contemporaries as capricious playing, or even caused them to suspect him of being in the service of the "black art." We who know him from his sketches understand him better. In a time in which the authority of the Church began to be substituted by that of antiquity and in which only theoretical investigation existed, he, the forerunner, or, better, the worthy competitor of Bacon and Copernicus, was necessarily isolated. When he dissected cadavers of horses and human beings, and built flying apparatus, or when he studied

Leonardo da Vinci

the nourishment of plants and their behavior toward poisons, he naturally deviated from the commentators of Aristotle and came nearer the despised alchemists, in whose laboratories the experimental investigations found some refuge during these unfavorable times.

The effect that this had on his paintings was that he disliked to handle the brush; he painted less and, what was more often the case, the things he began were mostly left unfinished; he cared less and less for the future fate of his works. It was this mode of working that was held up to him as a reproach by his contemporaries, to whom his attitude toward his art remained a riddle.

Many of Leonardo's later admirers have attempted to wipe off the stain of unsteadiness from his character. They maintained that what is blamed in Leonardo is a general characteristic of great artists. They said that even the energetic Michelangelo, who was absorbed in his art, left many incompleted works, which was as little due to his fault as to Leonardo's in the same case. Besides, some pictures were not as unfinished as he claimed, and what the laymen would call a masterpiece may still appear to the creator of the work of art as an unsatisfied embodiment of his intentions; he has a faint notion of a perfection which he despairs of reproducing in likeness. Least of all should the artist be held responsible for the fate which befalls his works.

As plausible as some of these excuses may sound, they nevertheless do not explain the whole state of affairs which we find in Leonardo. The painful struggle with the work, the final flight from it and the indifference to its future fate may be seen in many other artists, but this behavior is shown in Leonardo to the highest degree. Edm. Solmi cites (p. 12) the expression of one of his pupils: *"Pareva, che ad ogni ora tremasse, quando si poneva a dipingere, e però non diede mai fine ad alcuna cosa cominciata, considerando la grandezza dell'arte, tal che egli scorgeva errori in quelle cose, che ad altri parevano miracoli."* (It seems that he always trembled when he began to paint, and he therefore never brought to completion anything that he began; he was so impressed by the grandeur of art, that he detected faults in those things which appeared wonderful to others.)[4] His last pictures,

[4] Solmi: *La resurrezione dell' opera di Leonardo,* in the collected work, *Leonardo da Vinci, Conferenze Fiorentine,* Milan, 1910.

Leda, the Madonna di Sant' Onofrio, Bacchus, and St. John the Baptist, remained unfinished *"come quasi intervenne di tutte le cose sue."* Lomazzo,[5] who finished a copy of The Last Supper, refers in a sonnet to the familiar inability of Leonardo to finish his works:

> *"Protogen che il penel di sue pitture*
> *Non levava agguaglio il Vinci Divo,*
> *Di cui opera non è finita pure."*

The slowness with which Leonardo worked was proverbial. After the most thorough preliminary studies he painted The Last Supper for three years in the cloister of Santa Maria delle Grazie in Milan. One of his contemporaries, Matteo Bandelli, the writer of novels, who was then a young monk in the cloister, relates that Leonardo often ascended the scaffold very early in the morning and did not leave the brush out of his hand until twilight, never thinking of eating or drinking. Then days passed without putting his hand on it; sometimes he remained for hours before the painting and derived satisfaction from studying it by himself. At other times he came directly to the cloister

[5] Scognamiglio: *Ricerche e Documenti sulla giovinezza di Leonardo da Vinci.* Napoli, 1900.

A Study in Psychosexuality

from the palace of the Milanese Castle where he formed the model of the equestrian statue for Francesco Sforza, in order to add a few strokes with the brush to one of the figures, and then stopped immediately.[6] According to Vasari he worked for years on the portrait of Mona Lisa, the wife of the Florentine, de Gioconda, without being able to bring it to completion. This circumstance may also account for the fact that it was never delivered to the one who ordered it, but remained with Leonardo who took it with him to France.[7] Having been procured by King Francis I, it now forms one of the greatest treasures of the Louvre.

When one compares these reports about Leonardo's way of working with the evidence of the extraordinary number of sketches and studies left by him, one is bound altogether to reject the idea that traits of flightiness and unsteadiness exerted the slightest influence on Leonardo's relation to his art. On the contrary, one notices a very extraordinary absorption in work, a richness in possibilities in which a decision could be reached only hesitatingly, claims

[6] W. v. Seidlitz: *Leonardo da Vinci, der Wendepunkt der Renaissance,* 1909, Bd. I, p. 203.
[7] W. v. Seidlitz. l.c. Bd. II, p. 48.

Leonardo da Vinci

which could hardly be satisfied, and an inhibition in the execution which could not even be explained by the inevitable backwardness of the artist behind his ideal purpose. The slowness which was striking in Leonardo's works from the very beginning proved to be a symptom of his inhibition, a forerunner of his turning away from painting, which manifested itself later.[8] It was this slowness which decided the not undeserving fate of The Last Supper. Leonardo could not take kindly to the art of fresco painting, which demands quick work while the background is still moist. It was for this reason that he chose oil colors, the drying of which permitted him to complete the picture according to his mood and leisure. But these colors separated themselves from the background upon which they were painted and which isolated them from the brick wall; the blemishes of this wall and the vicissitudes to which the room was subjected seemingly contributed to the inevitable deterioration of the picture.[9]

The picture of the cavalry battle of Anghiari,

[8] W. Pater. *The Renaissance,* p. 107, The Macmillan Co., 1910. "But it is certain that at one period of his life he had almost ceased to be an artist."

[9] Cf. v. Seidlitz, Bd. I. *Die Geschichte der Restaurations- und Rettungsversuche.*

A Study in Psychosexuality

which, in competition with Michelangelo, he began to paint later on a wall of the Sala de Consiglio in Florence and which he also left in an unfinished state, seemed to have perished through the failure of a similar technical process. It seems here as if a peculiar interest, that of the experimenter, at first reinforced the artistic, only later to damage the art production.

The character of the man Leonardo evinces still some other unusual traits and apparent contradictions. Thus a certain inactivity and indifference seemed very evident in him. At a time when every individual sought to gain the widest latitude for his activity, which could not take place without the development of energetic aggression toward others, he surprised everyone by his quiet peacefulness, his shunning of all competition and controversies. He was mild and kind to all; he was said to have rejected a meat diet because he did not consider it just to rob animals of their lives; and one of his special pleasures was to buy caged birds in the market and set them free.[10] He condemned war and bloodshed and designated man not so much as

[10] Müntz. *Léonard de Vinci*, Paris, 1899, p. 18. (A letter of a contemporary from India to a Medici alludes to this peculiarity of Leonardo. Given by Richter: *The Literary Works of Leonardo da Vinci*.)

Leonardo da Vinci

the king of the animal world, but rather as the worst of the wild beasts.[11] But this effeminate delicacy of feeling did not prevent him from accompanying condemned criminals on their way to execution in order to study and sketch in his notebook their features, distorted by fear, nor did it prevent him from inventing the most cruel offensive weapons, and from entering the service of Cesare Borgia as chief military engineer. Often he seemed to be indifferent to good and evil, or he had to be measured with a special standard. He held a high position in Cesare's campaign, which gained for this most inconsiderate and most faithless of foes the possession of the Romagna. Not a single line of Leonardo's sketches betrays any criticism or sympathy in the events of those days. The comparison with Goethe during the French campaign cannot here be altogether rejected.

If a biographical effort really endeavors to penetrate the understanding of the psychic life of its hero, it must not, as happens in most biographies through discretion or prudery, pass over in silence the sexual activity or the sex peculiarity of the one examined. What we know

[11] F. Botazzi. *Leonardo biologo e anatomico. Conferenze Fiorentine,* p. 186, 1910.

A Study in Psychosexuality

about it in Leonardo is very little, but full of significance. In a period where there was a constant struggle between riotous licentiousness and gloomy asceticism, Leonardo presented an example of cool sexual rejection which one would not expect in an artist and a portrayer of feminine beauty. Solmi[12] cites the following sentence from Leonardo, showing his frigidity: "The act of procreation and everything that has any relation to it is so disgusting that human beings would soon die out if it were not a traditional custom, and if there were no pretty faces and sensuous dispositions." His posthumous works, which not only treat of the greatest scientific problems but also comprise the most guileless objects which to us do not seem worthy of so great a mind (an allegorical natural history, animal fables, witticisms, prophecies),[13] are chaste to a degree—one might say abstinent—that in a work of *belles-lettres* would excite wonder even today. They evade everything sexual so thoroughly, as if Eros alone who preserves everything living was no worthy material for the

---

[12] E. Solmi: *Leonardo da Vinci*. German translation by Emmi Hirschberg. Berlin, 1908.
[13] Marie Herzfeld: *Leonardo da Vinci der Denker, Forscher und Poet*. Second edition. Jena, 1906.

scientific impulse of the investigator.[14] It is known how frequently great artists found pleasure in giving vent to their phantasies in erotic and even grossly obscene representations; in contradistinction to this, Leonardo left only some anatomical drawings of the woman's internal genitals, the position of the child in the womb, etc.

It is doubtful whether Leonardo ever embraced a woman in love, nor is it known that he ever entertained an intimate spiritual relation with a woman, as in the case of Michelangelo and Vittoria Colonna. While he still lived as an apprentice in the house of his master, Verrocchio, he, with other young men, was accused of forbidden homosexual relations which ended in his acquittal. It seems that he came into this suspicion because he employed as a model a boy of evil repute.[15] When he was a

[14] His collected witticisms—*belle facezie*—which are not translated, may be an exception. Cf. Herzfeld, *Leonardo da Vinci*, p. 151.

[15] According to Scognamiglio (l.c., p. 49) reference is made to this episode in an obscure and even variously interpreted passage of the *Codex Atlanticus:* "*Quando io feci Domeneddio putto voi mi metteste in prigione, ora s'io lo fo grande, voi mi farete peggio.*" ("When I made Domeneddio as a youth you put me in prison, now if I should make him grown up you will do me worse.")

A Study in Psychosexuality

master he surrounded himself with handsome boys and youths whom he took as pupils. The last of these pupils, Francesco Melzi, accompanied him to France, remained with him until his death, and was named by him as his heir. Without sharing the certainty of his modern biographers, who naturally reject the possibility of a sexual relation between himself and his pupils as a baseless insult to this great man, it may be thought more probable by far that the affectionate relationships of Leonardo to the young men did not result in sexual activity. Nor should one attribute to him a high measure of sexual activity.

The peculiarity of this emotional and sexual life viewed in connection with Leonardo's double nature as an artist and investigator can be grasped only in one way. Of the biographers to whom psychological viewpoints are often very foreign, only one, Edm. Solmi, has to my knowledge approached the solution of the riddle. But a writer, Dmitri Sergewitsch Merejkowski, who selected Leonardo as the hero of a great historical novel, has based his delineation on such an understanding of this unusual man, and if not in dry words he gave unmistakable utterance to

Leonardo da Vinci

it in plastic expression in the manner of a poet.[16] Solmi judges Leonardo as follows: "But his unrequited wish to understand everything surrounding him, and to fathom with cold reflection the deepest secret of everything that is perfect, all that has condemned Leonardo's works to remain forever unfinished." [17] In an essay of the *Conferenze Fiorentine* the utterances of Leonardo are cited, which show his confession of faith and furnish the key to his character:

"Nessuna cosa si può amare nè odiare, se prima no si ha cognition di quella." [18]

That is: One has no right to love or to hate anything if one has not acquired a thorough knowledge of its nature. And the same is repeated by Leonardo in a passage of the *Treatise on the Art of Painting*, where he seems to defend himself against the accusation of irreligiousness:

"But such censurers might better remain silent. For that (action) is the manner of showing

---

[16] Merejkowski: *The Romance of Leonardo da Vinci*, translated from the Russian by Bernard Guilbert Guerney, The Modern Library, New York. It forms the second of the historical Trilogy entitled *Christ and Anti-Christ*, of which the first volume is *Julian the Apostate*, and the third volume is *Peter the Great and Alexei*.

[17] Solmi, l.c., p. 193.

[18] Filippo Botazzi, l.c., p. 193.

A Study in Psychosexuality

the workmaster so many wonderful things, and this is the way to love so great a discoverer. For verily, great love springs from great knowledge of the beloved object, and if you little know it, you will be able to love it only little or not at all." [19]

There is no psychological value in these utterances of Leonardo. What they maintain is obviously false, and Leonardo must have known this as well as we do. It is not true that people refrain from loving or hating until they have studied and become familiar with the nature of the object to whom they wish to give these affects. On the contrary they love impulsively; they are guided by emotional motives which have nothing to do with cognition; and their consequences are rather weakened by thought and reflection. Leonardo could have meant only that the love practiced by people is not the proper and unobjectionable kind, one should so love as to hold back the affect, and subject it to mental elaboration, and only after it has stood the test of the intellect should free play be given to it. And we thereby understand that he wishes to tell us that this was the case

[19] Marie Herzfeld: *Leonardo da Vinci, Traktat von der Malerei,* Jena, 1909 (Chap. I, p. 64).

with himself and that it would be worth the effort of everybody else to treat love and hatred as he himself does.

And it seems that in his case it was really so. His affects were controlled and subjected to the investigation impulse. He neither loved nor hated, but questioned himself whence does that arise which he was to love or hate, and what does it signify; and thus he was at first forced to appear indifferent to good and evil, to beauty and ugliness. During this work of investigation, love and hatred threw off their designs and uniformly changed into intellectual interest. As a matter of fact, Leonardo was not dispassionate; he did not lack the divine spark which is the mediate or immediate motive power—*il primo motore*—of all human activity. He only transmuted his passion into inquisitiveness. He then applied himself to study with that persistence, steadiness and profundity which comes from passion, and on the height of the psychic work, after the cognition was won, he allowed the long-checked affect to break loose and to flow off freely like a branch of a stream, after it has accomplished its work. At the height of his cognition, when he could examine a big part of the whole, he was seized with a feeling of pathos, and in ecstatic words he

A Study in Psychosexuality

praised the grandeur of that part of creation which he studied, or—in religious cloak—the greatness of the creator. Solmi has correctly divined this process of transformation in Leonardo. According to the quotation of such a passage, in which Leonardo celebrated the higher impulse of nature (*"O mirabile necessita . . ."*) he said: *"Tale trasfigurazione della scienza della natura in emozione, quasi direi, religiosa, è uno dei tratti caratteristici de' manoscritti vinciani, e si trova cento e cento volte espressa. . . ."* [20]

Leonardo was called the Italian Faust on account of his insatiable and indefatigable desire for investigation. But even if we disregard the fact that it is the possible retransformation of the desire for investigation into the joys of life which is presupposed in the Faust tragedy, one might venture to remark that Leonardo's system recalls Spinoza's mode of thinking.

The transformation of psychic motive power into the different forms of activity is perhaps as little convertible without loss, as in the case of physical forces. Leonardo's example teaches how

---

[20] "Such transfiguration of science and of nature into emotions, or one might say, religion, is one of the characteristic traits of da Vinci's manuscripts, which one finds expressed hundreds of times." Solmi: *La resurrezione,* etc., p. 11.

Leonardo da Vinci

many other things one must follow up in these processes. Not to love before one gains full knowledge of the thing loved presupposes a delay which is harmful. When one finally reaches cognition, he neither loves nor hates properly; one remains beyond love and hatred. One has investigated instead of having loved. It is perhaps for this reason that Leonardo's life was so much poorer in love than those of other great men and great artists. The storming passions of the soul-stirring and consuming kind, in which others experience the best part of their lives, seem to have missed him.

There are still other consequences when one follows Leonardo's dictum. Instead of acting and producing, one just investigates. He who begins to divine the grandeur of the universe and its needs readily forgets his own insignificant self. When one is struck with admiration and becomes truly humble, he easily forgets that he himself is a part of that living force, and that, according to the measure of his own personality, he has the right to make an effort to change that destined course of the world, the world in which the insignificant is no less wonderful and important than the great.

Solmi thinks that Leonardo's investigations

A Study in Psychosexuality

may have started with his art,[21] with his urge to investigate the attributes and laws of light, of color, of shades and of perspective. He wished to be sure of becoming a master in the imitation of nature and to be able to show the way to others. It is probable that already at that time he overestimated the value of this knowledge for the artist. Following the guide-rope of the painter's need, he was then driven further and further to investigate the objects of the art of painting, such as animals and plants, and the proportions of the human body, and to follow the path from their exterior to their interior structure and biological functions, which really also express themselves in their appearance and should be depicted in art. And, finally, he was pulled along by this overwhelming desire until the connection was torn from the demands of his art, so that he discovered the general laws of mechanics and devined the history of the stratification and fossilization of the Arno Valley, until he could enter in his book with capital letters the cognition: *Il sole non si move* (The sun does not move). His investigations were thus

[21] *La resurrezione,* etc., p. 8: "Leonardo placed the study of nature as a precept to painting . . . Later the passion for study became dominating; he no longer wished to acquire science for art, but science for science sake."

Leonardo da Vinci

extended over almost all realms of natural science, in every one of which he was a discoverer or at least a prophet and pathfinder.[22] However, his curiosity continued to be directed to the outer world; something kept him away from the investigation of the psychic life of men; there was little room for psychology in the *"Academia Vinciana,"* for which he drew very artistic and very complicated emblems.

When he later made the effort to return from his investigations to the art from which he started, he felt that he was disturbed by the new paths of his interest and by the changed nature of his psychic work. In the picture he was interested above all in a problem, and behind this one he saw emerging numerous other problems, just as he was accustomed in the endless and indeterminable investigations of natural history. He was no longer able to limit his demands, to isolate the work of art, and to tear it out from that great connection of which he knew it formed part. After the most exhausting efforts to bring to expression all that was in him, all that was connected with it in his thoughts, he was forced

[22] For an enumeration of his scientific attainments see Marie Herzfeld's interesting introduction (Jena, 1906), also in the essays of the *Conferenze Fiorentine,* 1910, and elsewhere.

A Study in Psychosexuality

to leave it unfinished, or to declare it incomplete.

The artist had once taken into his service the investigator to assist him; now the servant was stronger and suppressed his master.

When we find in the portrait of a person one single impulse very forcibly developed, as curiosity in the case of Leonardo, we look for the explanation in a special constitution, concerning the probable organic determination of which hardly anything is known. Our psychoanalytic studies of nervous people lead us to look for two other expectations which we would like to find verified in every case. We consider it probable that this very forcible impulse was already active in the earliest childhood of the person, and that its supreme sway was fixed by infantile impressions; and we further assume that originally it drew upon sexual motive powers for its reinforcement, so that it later can take the place of a part of the sexual life. Such person would then, e.g., investigate with that passionate devotion which another would give to his love, and he could investigate instead of loving. We would venture the conclusion of a sexual reinforcement not only in the impulse to investigate, but also in most other cases of special intensity of an impulse.

Leonardo da Vinci

Observation of daily life shows us that most persons have the capacity to direct a very tangible part of their sexual motive powers to their professional or business activities. The sexual impulse is particularly suited to yield such contributions because it is endowed with the capacity of sublimation, i.e., it has the power to exchange its nearest aim for others of higher value which are not sexual. We consider this process as proved, if the history of childhood or the history of the psychic development of a person shows that in his childhood this powerful impulse was in the service of sexual interest. We consider it a further corroboration if the sexual life of mature years evinces a striking stunting, as if a part of the sexual activity had now been replaced by the activity of the predominant impulse.

The application of these assumptions to the case of the predominant investigation-impulse seems to strike against special difficulties, for one is unwilling to admit that this serious impulse either exists in children or that they show any noteworthy sexual interest. However, these difficulties can easily be obviated. The untiring pleasure in questioning observed in little children demonstrates their curiosity, which is

A Study in Psychosexuality

puzzling to the grown-up, as long as he does not understand that all these questions are only circumlocutions, that they cannot come to an end, because the child wishes to substitute for them only one question which the child still does not put. When the child grows older and gains more understanding, this manifestation of curiosity suddenly disappears. But psychoanalytic investigation gives us a full explanation, in that it teaches us that many, perhaps most, children, at least the most gifted ones, go through a period beginning with the third year, which may be designated as the period of *infantile sexual investigation*. As far as we know, this curiosity is not awakened spontaneously in children of this age. It is aroused through the impression of an important experience, through the birth of a little brother or sister, or through fear of the same engendered by some outward experience, wherein the child sees a danger to his egotistic interests. The investigation directs itself to the question whence children come, as if the child were looking for means to guard against such an undesired event. We were astonished to find that the child refuses to give credence to the information imparted to it; thus it energetically rejects the mythological and very ingenious stork-fable,

Leonardo da Vinci

that its psychic independence dates from this act of disbelief, that it later often feels itself at serious variance with the grown-ups, and never forgives them for having been deceived of the truth on this occasion. It then investigates in its own way, and soon divines the sojourn of the child is in the mother's womb. Guided by the feelings of its own sexuality, the child formulates for itself theories about the origin of children—that they come from food, that they are born through the bowels—as well as the rôle of the father, which is difficult to fathom. Even at that time the child has a vague conception of the sexual act which he conceives as something hostile, as something violent. But as his own sexual constitution is not yet equal to the task of producing children, his investigation whence come children must also run aground and must be left in the lurch as unfinished. The impression of this failure at the first attempt of intellectual independence seems to be of a persevering and profoundly depressing nature.[23]

---

[23] For a corroboration of this improbable-sounding assertion see the "Analysis of the Phobia of a Five-year-old Boy," *Jahrbuch für Psychoanalytische und Psychopathologische Forschungen*, Bd. I, 1909, and the similar observation in Bd. II, 1910. In an essay concerning "Infantile Theories of Sex" (*Sammlungen kleiner Schriften zur Neurosenlehre*, p. 167,

A Study in Psychosexuality

If the period of infantile sexual investigation comes to an end through an impetus of energetic sexual repression, the early association with sexual interest may result in three different possibilities for the future fate of the investigation impulse. The investigation either shares the fate of the sexuality; the curiosity henceforth remains inhibited and the free activity of intelligence may become narrowed for life. This is especially favored shortly thereafter by education and powerful religious inhibitions. This is the type of neurotic inhibition. We know well that this so-acquired mental weakness furnishes effective support for the outbreak of a neurotic disease. In a second type the intellectual development is sufficiently strong to withstand the sexual repression pulling at it. Sometimes, after the disappearance of the infantile sexual investigation, it offers its support to the old association in order to elude sexual repression, and the suppressed sexual investigation comes back from the unconscious as compulsive reasoning. It is naturally distorted and not free, but forceful enough to sexualize even thought itself and to accentuate

---

Second Series, 1909), I wrote: "But this reasoning and doubting serves as a model for all later intellectual work in problems, and the first failure acts as a paralyzer for all times."

the intellectual operations with the pleasure and anxiety of the actual sexual processes. Here the investigation becomes sexual activity and often exclusively so; the feeling of settling the problem and of explaining things in the mind is put in place of sexual gratification. But the indeterminate character of the infantile investigation repeats itself also in the fact that this reasoning never ends, and that the desired intellectual feeling of the solution constantly recedes into the distance.

By virtue of a special disposition the third, which is the most rare and most perfect type, escapes the inhibition of thought and the compulsive reasoning. Also here sexual repression takes place, but it does not succeed in evincing a partial impulse of the sexual pleasure in the unconscious; instead the libido withdraws from the fate of the repression by being sublimated from the outset into curiosity, and by reinforcing the powerful investigation impulse. Here, too, the investigation becomes to some extent compulsive and substitutive of the sexual activity, but owing to the absolutely different psychic process behind it (sublimation in place of the emergence from the unconscious) the character of the neurosis fails to express itself; the subjec-

A Study in Psychosexuality

tion to the original complexes of the infantile sexual investigation disappears, and the impulse can freely put itself in the service of intellectual interest. To the sexual repression which made it so strong by contributing to it sublimated libido, it pays homage by avoiding all occupation with sexual themes.

In mentioning the concurrence in Leonardo of the powerful investigation impulse with the stunting of his sexual life, which was restricted to so-called ideal homosexuality, we are inclined to consider him a model example of our third type. The fact that after he utilized his infantile curiosity in the service of sexual interests he was then able to sublimate the greater part of his libido in the impulse to investigate; that would constitute the nucleus and the secret of his nature. But to be sure, the proof of this conception is not easy to produce. To do this we would have to have a view into the psychic development of his first childhood years, and it seems foolish to hope for such material when the reports concerning his life are so meager and so uncertain. Moreover, we are here dealing with information concerning situations which even persons of our own generation withhold from the attention of the observer.

Leonardo da Vinci

We know very little concerning Leonardo's youth. He was born in 1452 in the little city of Vinci between Florence and Empoli. He was an illegitimate child, which was surely not considered a great civic stain in that time. His father was Ser Piero da Vinci, a notary and descendant of a family of notaries and farmers, who took their name from the place Vinci; his mother was a certain Caterina, probably a peasant girl, who later married another native of Vinci. Nothing else about his mother appears in the life history of Leonardo. Only the writer Merejkowski believed that he had found some traces of her. The only definite information about Leonardo's childhood is furnished by a legal document from the year 1457, a Florentine tax register in which Vinci Leonardo is mentioned among the members of the family as a five-year-old illegitimate child of Ser Piero.[24] As the marriage of Ser Piero with Donna Albiera remained childless, the little Leonardo could be brought up in his father's house. He did not leave this house until he entered as apprentice—it is not known in what year—in the studio of Andrea del Verrocchio. In 1472 Leonardo's name could already be found in the register of the members of the "Compagnia dei Pittori." That is all.

[24] Scognamiglio, l.c., p. 15.

Two

As far as I know, Leonardo only once interspersed in his scientific descriptions a communication from his childhood. In a passage where he speaks about the flight of the vulture, he suddenly interrupts himself in order to follow up a memory from very early years which came to his mind.

"It seems that it had been destined before that I should occupy myself so thoroughly with the vulture, for it comes to my mind as a very early memory, when I was still in the cradle, a vulture came down to me, opened my mouth

with his tail and struck me many times with his tail against my lips." [1]

We have here an infantile memory, and, to be sure, of the strangest sort. It is strange on account of its content and because of the time of life in which it was fixed. That a person could retain a memory of his nursing period is perhaps not impossible, but it can in no way be taken as certain. But what this memory of Leonardo states, namely, that a vulture opened the child's mouth with its tail, sounds so improbable, so fabulous, that another view which puts an end to the two difficulties with one stroke appeals much more to our judgment. The scene of the vulture is not a memory of Leonardo, but a phantasy which he formed later, and transferred into his childhood. The childhood memories of people often have no different origin; as a matter of fact, they are surely not fixated from an experience like conscious memories from the time of maturity and then repeated, but they are brought up at a later period when childhood is

[1] *"Questo scriver si distintamente del nibbio par che sia mio destino, perchè nella mia prima ricordatione della mia infantia e mi parea che essendo io in oulla, che un nibbio venissi a me e mi aprissi la bocca colla sua coda e multe volte me percuotesse con tal coda dentro alle labbra."* Scognamiglio *Cod. Atlant.* F. 65 V.

A Study in Psychosexuality

already past; they are then changed, falsified and put in the service of later tendencies, so that in general they cannot be strictly differentiated from phantasies. Their nature will perhaps be best understood by recalling the manner in which history-writing originated among ancient nations. As long as the nation was small and weak it gave no thought to the writing of its history; it tilled the soil of its land, defended its existence against its neighbors by seeking to wrest land from them and endeavored to become rich. It was a heroic but unhistoric time. Then came another age, a period of self-realization in which one felt rich and powerful, and it was then that one experienced the need to discover whence one originated and how one developed. The history-writing which began by noting successively the experiences of the present, threw also its backward glance to the past; it gathered traditions and legends, interpreted what survived from olden times in ethics and customs, and thus created a history of past ages. It was inevitable that this pre-history was more the expressions of opinions and wishes of the present than a copy of the past. For much had escaped from the memory of its people; other things became distorted; some trace of the past was mis-

Leonardo da Vinci

understood and interpreted in the sense of the present; and, besides, one did not write history from motives of objective curiosity, but rather because one desired to impress his contemporaries, to stimulate and extol them, or to hold the mirror before them. The conscious memory of a person about the experiences of his maturity can now be in every way compared to that of history-writing, and his infantile memories, their origin and reliability, actually correspond to the tendentially corrected history of the primal period of a people which was compiled later.

If Leonardo's story of the vulture, which visited him in his cradle, is only a phantasy of later birth, one may think it hardly worth his while to give more time to it. To explain it, one could indeed be satisfied with his openly avowed tendency to occupy himself with the problem of bird flight which would thus lend an air of predetermined fate to this phantasy. But with this underestimation one would commit a similar injustice, as one who would simply ignore the material of legends, traditions and interpretations in the original history of a people. Notwithstanding all distortions and misunderstandings to the contrary, they still represent the reality of the past; they show what the people formed out of

A Study in Psychosexuality

the experiences of its primal past under the domination of once powerful and today still affective motives. And if these distortions could be traced back through the knowledge of all affective forces, one would surely discover the historic truth under this legendary material. The same holds true for the infantile reminiscences or for the phantasies of individuals. What a person thinks he recalls from his childhood is not of an indifferent nature. As a rule the memory remnants, which he himself does not understand, conceal invaluable evidences of the most important features of his psychic development. As the psychoanalytic technique affords us excellent means for bringing to light this concealed material, we shall venture the attempt to fill the gaps in the history of Leonardo's life through the analysis of his infantile phantasy. And should we not attain a satisfactory degree of certainty, we will have to console ourselves with the fact that so many other investigations about this great and mysterious man have met no better fate.

However, when we examine Leonardo's vulture-phantasy with the eyes of the psychoanalyst, then it does not appear strange to us very long; we recall that we have often found similar struc-

Leonardo da Vinci

tures in dreams, so that we can venture to translate this phantasy from its strange language into words that are universally understood. The translation, then, follows an erotic direction. Tail, "coda," is one of the most familiar symbols, as well as a substitutive designation of the male member, in Italian no less than in other languages. The situation contained in the phantasy, that a vulture opened the mouth of the child and forcefully belabored it with its tail, corresponds to the idea of *fellatio*, a sexual act in which the member is placed into the mouth of the other person. Strangely enough, this phantasy is altogether of a passive character; it resembles certain dreams and phantasies of women and of passive homosexuals (who play the feminine part in sexual relations).

Let the reader be patient for a while and not flare up with indignation and refuse to follow psychoanalysis because in its very first applications it leads to an unpardonable slander of the memory of a great and pure man. For it is quite certain that this indignation will never solve for us the meaning of Leonardo's childhood phantasy; on the other hand, Leonardo has unequivocally acknowledged this phantasy, and we shall therefore not relinquish the expectation—or if

A Study in Psychosexuality

you prefer the preconception—that like all psychic productions, such as dreams, visions and deliria, this phantasy, too, must have some meaning. Let us therefore lend our unprejudiced ears for a while to the psychoanalytic work, which after all has not yet spoken the last word.

The desire to take the male member into the mouth and suck it, which is commonly considered as one of the most disgusting of sexual perversions, is nevertheless a frequent occurrence among women of our time—and as shown in old sculptures was the same in earlier times—and in the state of being in love seems to lose entirely its disgusting character. The physician encounters phantasies based on this desire, even in women who did not come to the knowledge of the possibility of such sexual gratification by reading v. Krafft-Ebing's *Psychopathia Sexualis* or through other information. It seems that it is quite easy for women to produce spontaneously such wish-phantasies.[2] Investigation then teaches us that this situation, so forcibly condemned by custom, may be traced to the most harmless origin. It is nothing but the elaboration of another

[2] Cf. here the "Bruchstück einer Hysterieanalyse," in *Neurosenlehre*, Second Series, 1909. English tran. Strachey, *Collected Papers*, Vol. III, p. 13.

situation in which we all once felt comfort, namely, when we were in the suckling-age ("when I was still in the cradle"), and took the nipple of our mother's or wet-nurse's breast into our mouth to suck it. The organic impression of this first pleasure in our lives surely remains indelibly impregnated; when the child later learns to know the udder of the cow, which in function is a breast-nipple, but in shape and position on the abdomen resembles the penis, it obtains the primary basis for the later formation of that disgusting sexual phantasy.

We now understand why Leonardo displaced the memory of the supposed experience with the vulture to his nursing period. This phantasy conceals nothing more or less than a reminiscence of nursing—or being nursed—at the mother's breast, a scene both human and beautiful, which he, as well as other artists, undertook to depict with the brush in the form of the mother of God and her child. To be sure, we also wish to affirm something we do not as yet understand, that this reminiscence, equally significant for both sexes, was elaborated by the man Leonardo into a passive homosexual phantasy. For the present we shall leave aside the

A Study in Psychosexuality

question of the possible connection between homosexuality and suckling at the mother's breast, and merely recall that tradition actually designates Leonardo as a person of homosexual feelings. At the same time, it is immaterial whether that accusation against the youth Leonardo was justified or not. For it is not the actual activity but the nature of the feeling which decides for us whether we should attribute to any one the characteristic of homosexuality.

Another incomprehensible feature of Leonardo's infantile phantasy next claims our interest. We interpret the phantasy of being wet-nursed by the mother and find that the mother is replaced by a—vulture. Where does this vulture originate and how does he come into this place?

A thought now obtrudes itself which seems so remote that one is tempted to discard it. It is true that in the sacred hieroglyphics of the old Egyptians the mother is depicted by the picture of the vulture.[3] These Egyptians also worshiped a motherly deity, whose head was vulturelike, or who had many heads, of which at least one or

[3] Horapollo: *Hieroglyphica* 1, 11. Μητέρα δὲ γράφοντες . . . . . . γῦπα ξωγραφοῦσιν.

Leonardo da Vinci

two were that of a vulture.[4] The name of this goddess was pronounced *Mut;* we may question whether the sound similarity to our word mother (*Mutter*) is only accidental? So the vulture really has some connection with the mother; but of what help is that to us? Have we a right to attribute this knowledge to Leonardo when we know that François Champollion first succeeded in reading hieroglyphics between 1790-1832?[5]

It would also be of interest to us to discover in what way the old Egyptians came to choose the vulture as a symbol of motherhood. As a matter of fact, the religion and culture of Egyptians were subjects of scientific interest even to the Greeks and Romans, and long before we ourselves were able to read the Egyptian monuments, we had at our disposal some information about them from preserved works of classical antiquity. Some of these writings were from well-known authors like Strabo, Plutarch, Aminianus, Marcellus, while others bear unfamiliar names and are of uncertain origin and time, such as the hieroglyphics of Horapollo Nilus, and the

[4] Roscher: Ausf. *Lexicon der griechischen und römischen Mythologie.* Artikel Mut, II Bd., 1894-1897.—Lanzone. *Dizionario di Mitologia egizia.* Torino, 1882.
[5] H. Hartleben, *Champollion: Sein Leben und sein Werk,* 1906.

A Study in Psychosexuality

traditional book of oriental priestly wisdom which bears the godly name *Hermes Trismegistos*. From these sources we learn that the vulture was a symbol of motherhood because it was thought that this species of birds consisted only of females and no males.[6] The natural history of the ancients shows a counterpart to this limitation among the scarab beetles which were revered by the Egyptians as godly; among them no females were supposed to exist.[7]

But how does impregnation take place in vultures if only females exist? This is fully answered in a passage of *Horapollo*.[8] At a certain time these birds stop in the midst of their flight, open their vaginas and are impregnated by the wind.

Unexpectedly we have now reached a point where we can take something as quite probable which only shortly before we had to reject as absurd. It is quite possible that Leonardo was

[6] "γῦπα δὲ ἄρρενα οὐ φασιγένεσθαι ποτε, ἀιλὰ θηλείας ἁπάσας." cited by v. Römer. *Über die androgynische Idee des Lebens, Jahrb. F. Sexuelle Zwischenstufen*, V. 1903, p. 732.

[7] Plutarch: *Veluti scarabaeos mares tantum esse putarunt Aegyptii sic inter vultures mares non inveniri statuerunt.* (The Egyptians thought that there were only male scarab beetles but that no males existed among vultures.)

[8] *Horapollinis Niloi Hieroglyphica edidit Conradus Leemans Amstelodami*, 1835. The words referring to the sex of the vulture read as follows (p. 14): "μητέρα μὲν ἐπειδὴ ἄρρεν ἐν τούτῳ τῷ γένει τῶν ζώων οὐχ ὑπάρχει."

43

Leonardo da Vinci

well acquainted with the scientific fable, according to which the Egyptians represented the idea of mother with the picture of the vulture. He was an omnivorous reader whose interest comprised all spheres of literature and knowledge. In the *Codex Atlanticus* we find an index of all books which he possessed at a certain time,[9] as well as numerous notices about other books which he borrowed from friends, and, according to the excerpts which Fr. Richter[10] compiled from his drawings, we can hardly overestimate the extent of his reading. Among these books there was no lack of older as well as contemporary works treating of natural history. All these books were already in print at that time, and it so happens that Milan was the principal place of the young art of book printing in Italy.

When we proceed further we come upon a communication which may raise to a certainty the probability that Leonardo knew the vulture fable. The erudite editor and commentator of *Horapollo* remarked in connection with the text (p. 172) cited before: *Caeterum hanc fabulam de vulturibus cupide amplexi sunt Patres Ecclesiastici, ut ita argumento ex rerum natura*

[9] E. Müntz, l.c., p. 282.
[10] E. Müntz, l.c.

petito, refutarent eos, qui Virginis partum negabant; itaque apud omnes fere hujus rei mentio occurit.

Hence the fable of monosexuality and conception of the vulture by no means remained an indifferent anecdote as in the case of the analogous fable of the scarab beetle; for the Church fathers gladly accepted it in order to have it ready as an argument from natural history against those who doubted the virgin birth. If according to the best information from antiquity the vultures were directed to let themselves be impregnated by the wind, why should the same thing not have happened even once in a human female? It was because of this mode of reasoning that the Church fathers were "almost all" in the habit of repeating this vulture fable, and we can now hardly doubt that it also became known to Leonardo through this same powerful source.

The origin of Leonardo's vulture phantasy can now be depicted in the following manner: While he was once reading in a book of a Church father or in a work on natural science that vultures are all females and reproduce themselves without the co-operation of a male, a memory flashed through his mind which became transformed into the phantasy, but which wished to

Leonardo da Vinci

express that he too was such a vulture child, who had a mother but no father. An echo of the pleasure which he had once experienced at his mother's breast then associated itself to this phantasy in a manner as only such old impressions alone can manifest themselves. The allusion established by the authors to the idea of the holy virgin with the child, which was so dear to every artist, must have contributed to make this phantasy appear to him valuable and important. For this actually helped him to identify himself with the Christ child, the comforter and savior of not alone this one woman.

When we break up an infantile phantasy, we strive thereby to separate the real memory content from the later motives which modify and distort it. In the case of Leonardo we now think that we know the real content of the phantasy. The replacement of the mother by the vulture indicates that the child missed the father and felt himself alone with his mother. The fact of Leonardo's illegitimate birth fits in with his vulture phantasy; only because of it was he able to compare himself to a vulture child. But we have discovered as the next definite fact from his youth that at the age of five years he had already been received in his father's home; when

A Study in Psychosexuality

this took place, whether a few months following his birth or a few weeks before the taking of the tax assessment, is entirely unknown to us. The interpretation of the vulture phantasy then steps in and tells us that Leonardo did not spend the first decisive years of his life with his father and his stepmother but with his poor, forsaken real mother, so that he had time to miss his father. This still seems to be a rather meager and still a daring result of the psychoanalytic effort, but on further reflection it will grow in importance. We gain in certainty by mentioning the actual relations in Leonardo's childhood. According to the reports, his father, Ser Piero da Vinci, married the prominent Donna Albiera during the year of Leonardo's birth; it was due to the childlessness of this marriage that the boy owed his legalized reception into his father's or rather grandfather's house during his fifth year. However, it is not customary to offer an illegitimate offspring to a young wife's care at the beginning of her marriage when she is still expecting to be blessed with children. Years of disappointment must have elapsed before it was decided to adopt the probably handsomely developed illegitimate child, as a compensation for legitimate children who were vainly hoped for. It harmonizes best with the interpretation of the vulture-phantasy, if at least three or perhaps five years of Leonardo's life had elapsed before he was removed from his lonely mother to his father's home. But then it had already become too late. In the first three or four years of life impressions become fixed and modes of reactions are formed toward the outer world which can never be robbed of their importance by any later experiences.

If it is true that the incomprehensible childhood reminiscences and the person's phantasies based on them always bring out the most significant of his psychic development, then the fact, corroborated by the vulture phantasy, that Leonardo passed the first years of his life alone with his mother must have been a most decisive influence on the formation of his inner life. Under the effect of this constellation it could not have been otherwise than that the child, who in his young life encountered one problem more than other children, should have begun to ponder very passionately over this riddle and thus should have become an investigator early in life. For he was tortured by the great questions where do children come from and what has the father to do with their origin. The vague knowledge of this connection between his in-

A Study in Psychosexuality

vestigation and his childhood history has later drawn from him the exclamation that it was destined that he should deeply occupy himself with the problem of the bird's flight, for already in his cradle he had been visited by a vulture. To trace the curiosity which is directed to the flight of the bird to the infantile sexual investigation will be a later task which will not be difficult to accomplish.

Three

The element of the vulture represents to us the real memory content in Leonardo's childhood phantasy; the association into which Leonardo himself placed his phantasy threw a bright light on the importance of this content for his later life. In continuing the work of interpretation we now encounter the strange problem: why this memory content was elaborated into a homosexual situation. The mother who nursed the child, or rather from whom the child suckled, was transformed into a vulture which stuck its tail into the child's mouth. We maintain that the "coda" (tail) of the vulture, following the common substituting usages of language, cannot sig-

A Study in Psychosexuality

nify anything else but a male genital or penis. But we do not understand how the phantastic activity came to furnish precisely this maternal bird with the mark of masculinity, and in view of this absurdity we become confused at the possibility of reducing this phantastic structure to rational sense.

However, we must not despair. How many seemingly absurd dreams have we not forced to give up their sense! Why should it become more difficult to accomplish this in a childhood phantasy than in a dream?

Let us remember the fact that it is not good to find one isolated peculiarity, and let us hasten to add another to it which is still more striking.

The vulture-headed goddess *Mut* of the Egyptians, a figure of altogether impersonal character, as expressed by Drexel in Roscher's lexicon, was often fused with other maternal deities of more vivid individuality like Isis and Hathor, but she retained thereby her separate existence and reverence. It was especially characteristic of the Egyptian pantheon that the individual gods did not perish in this syncretism. Besides the composition of deities the simple divine image remained in her independence. In most representations the vulture-headed ma-

Leonardo da Vinci

ternal deity was formed by the Egyptians in a phallic manner;[1] her body which was distinguished as feminine by its breasts also bore the masculine member in a state of erection.

The goddess *Mut* thus evinced the same union of maternal and paternal characteristics as in Leonardo's vulture phantasy. Should we explain this coincidence by the assumption that Leonardo knew from reading his books the androgynous nature of the maternal vulture? Such possibility is more than questionable; it seems that the sources accessible to him contained nothing of this remarkable determination. It is more likely that the agreement should here as there be traced to a common, affective and still-unknown motive.

Mythology can teach us that the androgynous formation, the union of masculine and feminine sex characteristics, did not belong to the goddess *Mut* alone but also to other deities such as Isis and Hathor, but in the latter perhaps only insofar as they possessed also a motherly nature and became fused with the goddess *Mut*.[2] It teaches us further that other Egyptian deities, such as Neith of Sais out of whom the Greek Athene

[1] See the illustrations in Lanzone, l.c., T. CXXXVI-VIII.
[2] Römer, l.c.

A Study in Psychosexuality

was later formed, were originally conceived as androgynous or dihermaphroditic, and that the same held true for many of the Greek gods, especially of the Dionysian circle, as well as for Aphrodite who was later restricted to a feminine love deity. Mythology may also offer the explanation that the phallus which was added to the feminine body was meant to denote the creative primitive force of nature, and that all these hermaphroditic deistic formations express the idea that only a union of the masculine and feminine elements can result in a worthy representation of divine perfection. But none of these observations explain the psychological riddle, namely, that the phantasy of men takes no offense at the fact that a figure which was to embody the essence of the mother should be provided with the mark of the masculine power which is the opposite of motherhood.

The explanation comes from the infantile sexual theories. There really was a time in which the male genital was found to be compatible with the representation of the mother. When the male child first directs his curiosity to the riddle of the sexual life, he is dominated by the interest for his own genitals. He finds this part of the body too valuable and too important to be-

Leonardo da Vinci

lieve that it would be missing in other persons to whom he feels such a resemblance. As he cannot divine that there is still another equally valuable type of genital formation he must grasp the assumption that all persons, also women, possess such a member as he. This preconception is so firm in the youthful investigator that it is not destroyed even by the first observation of the genitals in little girls. His perception naturally tells him that there is something different here than in him, but he is unable to admit to himself as the content of this perception that he cannot find this member in girls. That this member may be missing is to him a dismal and unbearable thought, and he therefore seeks to reconcile it by deciding that it also exists in girls but it is still very small and that it will grow later.[3] If this expectation does not appear to be fulfilled on later observation, he has at his disposal another way of escape. The member also existed in the little girl but it was cut off and in its place remained a wound. This progress in the theory already makes use of his own painful experience; he was threatened in the meantime that this important organ will be taken away

---

[3] Cf. the observations in the *Jahrbuch für Psychoanalytische und Psychopathologische Forschungen*, Vol. I, 1909.

A Study in Psychosexuality

from him if it will form too much of an interest for his occupation. Under the influence of this threat of castration he now reinterprets his conception of the female genital; henceforth he will tremble for his masculinity, but at the same time he will look with contempt upon those unhappy creatures upon whom, in his opinion, this cruel punishment had already been visited.

Before the child came under the domination of the castration complex, at the time when he still held the woman at her full value, he began to manifest an intensive desire to look, as an erotic activity of his impulse. He wished to see the genitals of other persons, originally probably because he wished to compare them with his own. The erotic attraction which emanated from the person of his mother soon reached its height in the longing to see her genital, which he believed to be a penis. With the cognition acquired only later that the woman has no penis, this longing often becomes transformed into its opposite and gives place to disgust, which in the years of puberty may become the cause of psychic impotence, of misogyny and of lasting homosexuality. But the fixation on the once so vividly desired object, the penis of the woman, leaves ineradicable traces in the psychic life of the child, which has gone through that fragment of infantile sexual investigation with particular thoroughness. The fetish-like reverence for the feminine foot and shoe seems to take the foot only as a substitutive symbol for the once revered and since then missed member of the woman. The "braid-snippers," without knowing it, play the part of persons who perform the act of castration on the female genital.[4]

One will not gain any correct understanding of the activities of the infantile sexuality and probably will consider these communications unworthy of belief, as long as one does not relinquish the attitude of our cultural depreciation of the genitals and of the sexual functions in general. To understand the infantile psychic life one has to look to analogies from primitive times. For a long series of generations we have been in the habit of considering the genitals or *pudenda* as objects of shame, and in the case of more successful sexual repression as objects of disgust. The majority of those living today only reluctantly obey the laws of propagation, feeling thereby that their human dignity is thereby

[4] This sadistic perversion which was quite frequently noticed before most of our women discarded their long hair is nowadays rarely encountered. (Translator)

A Study in Psychosexuality

offended and degraded. What exists among us of other views of the sexual life has retreated to the coarse remnants of the lower social strata; among the higher and more refined people it is concealed as something culturally inferior, and dares to assert itself only under the embittered admonition of a guilty conscience. It was quite different in the primitive times of the human race. From the laborious collections of students of civilization one gains the conviction that the genitals were originally the pride and hope of living beings; they enjoyed divine worship, and the divine nature of their functions was transported to all newly acquired activities of mankind. Through sublimation of its essential elements there arose innumerable god-figures, and later when the official relations between religion and sexual activity were hidden from the general consciousness, secret cults labored to preserve it alive among a number of initiates. In the course of cultural development it finally happened that so much godliness and holiness had been extracted from sexuality that the exhausted remnant fell into contempt. But considering the indestructibility which is in the nature of all psychic impressions one need not wonder that even the most primitive forms of genital worship could be demonstrated until quite recent times, and that language, customs and superstitions of present-day humanity contain the remnants of all phases of this course of development.[5]

Important biological analogies have taught us that the psychic development of the individual is a short repetition of the course of development of the race, and we shall therefore not find improbable what the psychoanalytic investigation of the child's psyche asserts concerning the infantile estimation of the genitals. The infantile assumption of the maternal penis is thus the common source of origin for the androgynous formation of the maternal deities like the Egyptian goddess *Mut* and the vulture's "coda" (tail) in Leonardo's childhood phantasy. As a matter of fact, it is only through misunderstanding that these deistic representations are designated hermaphroditic in the medical sense of the word. In none of them is there a union of the true genitals of both sexes as they are united in some deformed beings to the disgust of every human eye; but besides the breast as a mark of motherhood there is also the male member, just as it existed in the first imagination of the child

[5] Cf. Richard Payne Knight: *The Cult of Priapus.*

A Study in Psychosexuality

about his mother's body. Mythology has retained for the faithful this revered and very early fancied bodily formation of the mother. The emphasis given to the vulture-tail in Leonardo's phantasy we can now translate as follows: At that time when I directed my tender curiosity to my mother I still attributed to her a genital like my own. Another evidence of Leonardo's precocious sexual investigation, which in our opinion became decisive for his entire life.

A brief reflection now admonishes us that we should not be satisfied with the explanation of the vulture-tail in Leonardo's childhood phantasy. It seems as if it contained more than we as yet understand. For its more striking feature really consisted in the fact that the nursing at the mother's breast was transformed into being nursed, that is, into a passive act which thus gives the situation an undoubted homosexual character. Mindful of the historical probability that Leonardo behaved in life as a homosexual in feeling, the question obtrudes itself whether this phantasy does not point to a casual connection between Leonardo's childhood relations to his mother and the later manifest, if only ideal, homosexuality. We would not venture to draw such conclusion from Leonardo's disfigured reminiscence, were it not for the fact that we know from our psychoanalytic investigation of homosexual patients that such a relation exists; indeed, it really is an intimate and necessary relation.

Homosexual men who have started in our times an energetic action against the legal restrictions of their sexual activity are fond of representing themselves through theoretical spokesmen as evincing a sexual variation, which may be distinguished from the very beginning, as an intermediate stage of sex or as "a third sex." In other words, they maintain that they are men who are forced by organic determinants originating in the germ to find that pleasure in the man which they cannot feel in the woman. As much as one would wish to subscribe to their demands out of humane considerations, one must nevertheless exercise reserve regarding their theories which were formulated without regard for the psychogenesis of homosexuality. Psychoanalysis offers the means to fill this gap and to put to test the assertions of the homosexuals. It is true that psychoanalysis fulfilled this task in only a small number of people, but all investigation thus far undertaken brought the same surprising

A Study in Psychosexuality

results.[6] In all our male homosexuals there was a very intensive erotic attachment to a feminine person, as a rule to the mother, which was manifest in the very first period of childhood and later entirely forgotten by the individual. This attachment was produced or favored by too much love from the mother herself, but was also furthered by the retirement or absence of the father during the childhood period. Sadger emphasizes the fact that the mothers of his homosexual patients were often man-women, or women with energetic traits of character who were able to crowd out the father from the place allotted to him in the family. I have sometimes observed the same thing, but I was more impressed by those cases in which the father was absent from the beginning or disappeared early so that the boy was altogether under feminine influence. It seems almost that the presence of a strong father would assure for the son the proper decision in the selection of his object from the opposite sex.

Following this primary stage, a transformation takes place whose mechanisms we know but

[6] Prominently among those who undertook these investigations are I. Sadger, whose results I can essentially corroborate from my own experience. I am also aware that Stekel of Vienna, Ferenczi of Budapest, and Brill of New York came to the same conclusions.

Leonardo da Vinci

whose motive forces we have not yet grasped. The love of the mother cannot continue to develop consciously so that it merges into repression. The boy represses the love for the mother by putting himself in her place, by identifying himself with her, and by taking his own person as a model through the similarity of which he is guided in the selection of his love object. He thus becomes homosexual; as a matter of fact, he returns to the stage of autoerotism, for the boys whom the growing adult now loves are only substitutive persons or revivals of his own childish person, whom he loves in the same way as his mother loved him. We say that he finds his love object on the road to narcissism, for the Greek legend called a boy Narcissus to whom nothing was more pleasing than his own mirrored image, and who became transformed into a beautiful flower of this name.

Deeper psychological discussions justify the assertion that the person who becomes homosexual in this manner remains fixed in his unconscious on the memory picture of his mother. By repressing the love for his mother he conserves the same in his unconscious and henceforth remains faithful to her. When as a lover he seems to pursue boys, he really thus runs away

A Study in Psychosexuality

from women who could cause him to become disloyal to his mother. Through direct observation of individual cases we could demonstrate that he who is seemingly receptive only of masculine stimuli is in reality influenced by the charms emanating from women just like a normal person, but each and every time he hastens to transfer the stimulus he received from the woman to a male object, and in this manner he repeats again and again the mechanism through which he acquired his homosexuality.

It is far from our intention to exaggerate the importance of these explanations concerning the psychogenesis of homosexuality. It is quite clear that they are in crass opposition to the official theories of the homosexual spokesmen, but we are aware that these explanations are not sufficiently comprehensive to render possible a final explanation of the problem. What one calls homosexual for practical purposes may have its origin in a variety of psychosexual inhibiting processes, and the process recognized by us is perhaps only one among many, and has reference only to one type of "homosexuality." We must also admit that the number of cases of our homosexual type in which the conditions postulated by us are demonstrable exceeds by far

Leonardo da Vinci

those cases in which the derived effect really appears. Hence we too cannot reject the co-operation of unknown constitutional factors from which the whole of homosexuality was formerly derived. As a matter of fact, there would have been no occasion for entering into the psychogenesis of the form of homosexuality studied by us if there had not been a strong presumption that Leonardo, from whose vulture-phantasy we started, really belonged to this one type of homosexuality.

As little as is known concerning the sexual behavior of the great artist and investigator, we must still trust to the probability that the testimonies of his contemporaries did not go far astray. In the light of this tradition he appears to us as a man whose sexual need and activity were extraordinarily low, as if a higher striving had raised him above the common animal need of mankind. It may be open to doubt whether he ever sought direct sexual gratification, and in what manner, or whether he could dispense with it altogether. We are justified, however, to look also in him for those emotional streams which imperatively force others to the sexual act, for we cannot imagine a human psychic life in whose development the sexual desire in the

A Study in Psychosexuality

broadest sense, the libido, has not had its share, whether the latter has withdrawn itself far from the original aim or whether it was detained from being put into execution.

Anything but traces of an unchanged sexual tendency we need not expect in Leonardo. These point however to one direction and thus permit us to count him among homosexuals. It has always been emphasized that he took as his pupils only strikingly handsome boys and youths. He was kind and considerate toward them; he cared for them and nursed them himself when they were ill, just as a mother nurses her children, as his own mother might have cared for him. As he selected them for their beauty rather than for their talent, none of them—Cesare da Sesto, G. Boltraffio, Andrea Salaino, Francesco Melzi or the others—ever became a prominent artist. Most of them could not make themselves independent of their master and disappeared after his death without leaving a more definite physiognomy to the history of art. The others who by their productions earned the right to call themselves his pupils, as Luini and Bazzi, nicknamed Sodoma, he probably did not know personally.

We realize that we shall have to face the objection that Leonardo's behavior toward his

Leonardo da Vinci

pupils surely had nothing to do with sexual motives, and permits no conclusion as to his sexual peculiarity. Against this we wish to assert with all caution that our conception explains some strange features in the master's behavior which otherwise would have remained enigmatical. Leonardo kept a diary; he made entries in his small hand, written from right to left which were meant only for himself. Remarkably enough in this diary he addressed himself with "thou": "Learn from master Lucca the multiplication of roots." [7] "Let master d'Abacco show thee the square of the circle." [8] Or on the occasion of a journey he entered in his diary:

"I am going to Milan to look after the affairs of my garden . . . Order two pack-sacks to be made. Ask Boltraffio to show thee his turning-lathe and let him polish a stone on it.—Leave the book to master Andrea il Todesco." [9] Or, a resolution of quite a different significance: "Thou must show in thy treatise that the earth

---

Edm. Solmi: *Leonardo da Vinci*, German translation, p. 152.
[8] Solmi, l.c., p. 203.
[9] Leonardo thus behaves like one who was in the habit of making a daily confession to another person whom he now replaced by his diary. For an assumption as to who this person may have been, see Merejkowski, p. 309.

A Study in Psychosexuality

is a star, like the moon or resembling it, and thus prove the nobility of our world."[10]

In this diary, which like the diaries of other mortals often skim over the most important events of the day with only a few words or ignore them altogether, one finds a few entries which on account of their peculiarity are cited by all of Leonardo's biographers. They show notations referring to the master's petty expenses, which are recorded with painful exactitude as if coming from a pedantic and strictly parsimonious family father, whereas any references to expenditures of greater sums are lacking, and there is nothing to show that the artist was versed in household management. One of these notes refers to a new cloak which he bought for his pupil, Andrea Salaino:[11]

Silver brocade	*Lira*	*15*	*Soldi*	*4*
Crimson velvet for trimming	"	*9*	"	*0*
Braid	"	*0*	"	*9*
Buttons	"	*0*	"	*12*

Another very detailed notice gives all the expenses he incurred through the bad qualities

[10] M. Herzfeld: *Leonardo da Vinci*, 1906, p. 141.
[11] The wording is that of Merejkowski, l.c., p. 137.

Leonardo da Vinci

and thieving propensities of another pupil: "On 21st day of April, 1490, I started this book and began again the horse.[12] Jacomo came to me on Magdalene day, 1490, at the age of ten years (marginal note: thievish, mendacious, willful, gluttonous). On the second day I ordered for him two shirts, a pair of pants and a jacket, and as I put the money aside to pay for the things named he stole the money from my purse, and it was never possible to make him confess, although I was absolutely sure of it (marginal note: 4 Lira . . .)." So the report continues concerning the misdeeds of the little boy and concludes with the expense account: "In the first year, a cloak, Lira 2; 6 shirts, Lira 4; 3 jackets, Lira 6; 4 pair of socks, Lira 7, etc." [13]

Leonardo's biographers, to whom nothing was further than to solve the riddle in the psychic life of their hero from these slight weaknesses and peculiarities, were wont to remark in connection with these peculiar accounts that they emphasized the kindness and consideration of the master for his pupils. They forget thereby that it is not Leonardo's behavior that needs an explanation, but the fact that he left us these

[12] The equestrian monument of Francesco Sforza.
[13] The full wording is found in Herzfeld, l.c., p. 45.

A Study in Psychosexuality

testimonies of it. As it is impossible to ascribe to him the motive of smuggling into our hands proof of his kindness, we must assume that another, affective motive induced him to note this. It is not easy to conjecture what this motive was, and we could not give any if not for another account found among Leonardo's papers, which throws a brilliant light on these peculiarly petty notices about his pupils' clothes, and others of a kind:[14]

Burial expenses following the death of Caterina........ 27 florins
2 pounds wax............. 18 "
Cataphalc .... 12 "
For the transportation and erection of the cross...... 4 "
Pall bearers .... 8 "

[14] Merejkowski, l.c.—As a disappointing illustration of the vagueness of the information concerning Leonardo's intimate life, meager as it is, I mention the fact that the same expense account is given by Solmi with considerable variation (German translation, p. 104). The most serious difference is the substitution of florins by soldi. One may assume that in this account florins do not mean the old "gold florins," but those used at a later period which amounted to 1⅔ lira or 33½ soldi. Solmi represents Caterina as a servant who had taken care of Leonardo's household for a certain time. The source from which the two versions of this account were taken was not accessible to me.

To 4 priests and 4 clerks....   20   "
Ringing of bells...........   2   "
To grave diggers..........   16   "
For the approval—to the officials   1   "

To sum up............ 108 florins
Previous expenses:
  To the doctor.... 4 florins
  For sugar and candles 12   "

                       16 florins

Sum total .... 124 florins

The writer Merejkowski is the only one who tells us who this Caterina was. From two other brief entries he concludes that she was the mother of Leonardo, the poor peasant woman from Vinci, who came to Milan in 1493 to visit her son then forty-one years old. While on this visit she fell ill and was taken to the hospital by Leonardo, and following her death she was buried by her son with such a sumptuous funeral.[15]

This conclusion of the writer of psychological romances is not provable, but it can lay claim to

---

[15] "Caterina arrived in July, 1493."—"Giovannina—a fairy-like face—inquire of Caterina in the hospital."

A Study in Psychosexuality

so many inner probabilities, and agrees so well with everything we know besides about Leonardo's emotional activity, that I cannot refrain from accepting it as correct. Leonardo was able to constrain his feelings under the yoke of investigation and to inhibit their free expression, but even in him there were cases in which the suppressed material strained for free expression, and one of these was the death of his mother whom he once loved so ardently. Through this account of the burial expenses he represents to us the mourning of his mother in an almost unrecognizable distortion. We wonder how such a distortion could have come about, and we certainly cannot grasp it when viewed under normal mental processes. But similar mechanisms are familiar to us from abnormal neurotic conditions, and especially from the so-called compulsion neuroses. Here one can observe how expressions of very intensive feelings have been displaced by trivial and even foolish performances. The opposing forces succeeded in debasing the expression of these repressed feelings to such an extent that one is forced to estimate the intensity of these feelings as extremely unimportant, but the imperative compulsion with which these insignificant acts express themselves

Leonardo da Vinci

betrays the real force of the feelings which are rooted in the unconscious, and which consciousness wishes to disavow. Only by bearing in mind the mechanisms of compulsion neurosis can one explain Leonardo's account of the funeral expenses of his mother. In his unconscious he was still tied to her as in childhood, by erotically tinged feelings. The resistance of the repression of this childhood love which appeared later stood in the way of erecting to her in his diary a different and more dignified monument, but what resulted as a compromise of this neurotic conflict had to be put in operation, and hence the account was entered in the diary and came to the knowledge of posterity as something incomprehensible.

It is not venturing far to transfer the insight gained from the funeral expenses to the accounts dealing with his pupils. Accordingly we would say that here too we deal with a case in which Leonardo's meager remnants of libidinal feelings compulsively construed a distorted expression. The mother and the pupils, the very images of his own boyish beauty, would be his sexual objects—as far as his sexual repression dominating his nature would allow such manifestations—and the compulsion to note with painful

A Study in Psychosexuality

circumstantiality his expenses on their behalf, would designate the strange betrayal of his rudimentary conflicts. From this we would conclude that Leonardo's love-life really belonged to that type of homosexuality, the psychic development of which we were able to disclose, and the appearance of the homosexual situation in his vulture-phantasy thus becomes comprehensible to us, for it states nothing other than what we have asserted before concerning that type. It requires the following interpretation: Through the erotic relations to my mother I became a homosexual.[16]

[16] The manner of expression through which the repressed libido could manifest itself in Leonardo, such as circumstantiality and marked interest in money, belong to those traits of character which emanate from anal eroticism. Cf. *Character und Analerotik* in the second series of my *Sammlungen kleiner Schriften zur Neurosenlehre,* 1909, also Brill's and Jones' works on *Anal Eroticism and Character.*

Four

The vulture phantasy of Leonardo still absorbs our interest. In words which only too plainly allude to a sexual act ("and has many times struck against my lips with his tail"), Leonardo emphasizes the intensity of the erotic relations between the mother and the child. A second memory content of the phantasy can readily be conjectured from the association of the activity of the mother (of the vulture) with the accentuation of the oral zone. We can translate it: "My mother has pressed on my mouth innumerable passionate kisses." The phantasy is composed of the memories being nursed and of being kissed by the mother.

A Study in Psychosexuality

A kindly nature has bestowed upon the artist the capacity to express in artistic productions his most secret psychic feelings hidden even from himself, which powerfully grips outsiders, strangers to the artist, without their knowing whence this emotivity comes. Should there be no evidence in Leonardo's works of that which his memory retained as the strongest impression of his childhood? One must expect it. However, when one considers what profound transformations an impression of an artist has to experience before it can add its contribution to the work of art, one is obliged to moderate considerably his expectation of demonstrating something definite. This is especially true in the case of Leonardo.

He who thinks of Leonardo's paintings will recall the remarkably fascinating and puzzling smile which he enchanted on the lips of all his feminine figures. It is a fixed smile on elongated sinuous lips, which is considered characteristic of him and is preferentially designated as "Leonardesque." In the singular and beautiful visage of the Florentine, Mona Lisa del Gioconda, it has produced the greatest effect on the spectators and even perplexed them. This smile was in need of an interpretation, and received many of the most varied kinds, but none of them was con-

Leonardo da Vinci

sidered satisfactory. As Gruyer puts it: *"Voilà quatre siècles bientôt que Mona Lisa fait perdre la tête à ceux qui parlent d'elle après l'avoir longtemps regardée."* ("It is almost four centuries since Mona Lisa causes all those to lose their heads who speak of her, after they have looked upon her for a long time.")[1]

Muther states:[2] "What fascinates the spectator is the demoniacal charm of this smile. Hundreds of poets and writers have written about this woman, who now seems to smile upon us seductively and now to stare coldly and soullessly into space, but nobody has solved the riddle of her smile, nobody has interpreted her thoughts. Everything, even the scenery, is mysterious and dream-like, trembling as if in the sultriness of sensuality."

The idea that two diverse elements were united in the smile of Mona Lisa has been felt by many critics. They therefore recognize in the play of features of the beautiful Florentine lady the most perfect representation of the contrasts dominating the love-life of the woman, namely, reserve and seduction, most submissive tenderness and the indifferent craving, which confront

[1] Seidlitz: *Leonardo da Vinci*, Bd. II, p. 280.
[2] *Geschichte der Malerei*, Bd. I, p. 314.

the man as a strange and consuming sensuality. Müntz[3] expresses himself in this manner: *"On sait quelle énigme indéchiffrable et passionant Mona Lisa Gioconda ne cesse depuis bientôt quatre siècles, de proposer aux admirateurs pressé devant elle. Jamais artiste (j'emprunte la plume de délicat écrivain qui se cache sous le pseudonyme de Pierre de Corlay) a-t-il traduit ainsi l'essence même de la féminité: tendresse et coquetterie, pudeur et sourde volupté, tout le mystère d'un coeur qui se réserve, d'un cerveau qui réfléchit, d'un personnalité qui se garde et ne livre d'elle-même que son rayonment. . . ."* ("One knows what indecipherable and fascinating enigma Mona Lisa Gioconda has been putting for nearly four centuries to the admirers who crowd around her. No artist [I borrow the expression of the delicate writer who hides himself under the pseudonym of Pierre de Corlay] has ever translated in the manner the very essence of femininity: the tenderness and coquetry, the modesty and quiet voluptuousness, the whole mystery of the heart which holds itself aloof, of a brain which reflects, and of a personality who watches itself and yields nothing from herself except radiance. . . .") The Italian Angelo

[3] l.c., p. 417.

Conti[4] saw the picture in the Louvre illumined by a ray of the sun and expressed himself as follows: *"La donna sorrideva in una calma regale: i suoi instinti di conquista, di ferocia, tutta l'eredita della specie, la voluntà della seduzione e dell' agguato, la grazia del inganno, la bontà che cela un proposito crudele, tutto cio appariva alternativamente e scompariva dietro il velo ridente, e si fondera nel poema del suo sorriso. . . . Buona e malvaggia, crudele e compassionevole, graziosa e felina, ella rideva. . . ."* ("The woman smiled with a royal calmness, her instincts of conquest, of ferocity, the entire heredity of the species, the will of seduction and ensnaring, the charm of the deceiver, the kindness which conceals a cruel purpose, all that appeared and disappeared alternately behind the laughing veil and melted into the poem of her smile . . . Good and evil, cruelty and compassion, graceful and cat-like, she laughed . . .")

Leonardo devoted four years to the painting of this picture, perhaps from 1503 until 1507, during his second sojourn in Florence when he was about the age of fifty years. According to Vasari he applied the choicest artifices in order to divert the lady during the sittings and to hold

[4] A. Conti: *Leonardo pittore, Conferenze Fiorentine,* l.c., p. 93.

A Study in Psychosexuality

that smile firmly on her features. Of all the gracefulness that his brush reproduced on the canvas at that time the picture preserves but very little in its present state. During its production it was considered the highest that art could accomplish; it is certain, however, that it did not satisfy Leonardo himself, that he pronounced it as unfinished and did not deliver it to the one who ordered it, but took it with him to France where his benefactor, Francis I, acquired it for the Louvre.

Let us leave the physiognomic riddle of Mona Lisa unsolved, and let us note the unequivocal fact that her smile fascinated the artist no less than all spectators for these 400 years. This captivating smile had thereafter returned in all of his pictures and in those of his pupils. As Leonardo's Mona Lisa was a portrait, we cannot assume that he has added to her face a trait of his own, so difficult to express, which she herself did not possess. It seems, we cannot help but believe, that he found this smile in his model and became so charmed by it that from now on he endowed it on all the free creations of his phantasy. This obvious conception is, e.g., expressed by A. Konstantinowa in the following manner: [5]

[5] l.c., 45.

Leonardo da Vinci

"During the long period in which the master occupied himself with the portrait of Mona Lisa del Gioconda, he entered into the physiognomic delicacies of this feminine face with such sympathy of feeling that he transferred these features, especially the mysterious smile and the peculiar glance, to all faces which he later painted or drew. The mimic peculiarity of Gioconda can even be perceived in the picture of John the Baptist in the Louvre. But above all they are distinctly recognized in the features of Mary in the picture of St. Anne of the Louvre."

But the case could have been different. The need for a deeper reason for the fascination which the smile of Gioconda exerted on the artist from which he could not rid himself has been felt by more than one of his biographers. W. Pater, who sees in the picture of Mona Lisa the embodiment of the entire erotic experience of modern man, and discourses so excellently on "that unfathomable smile always with a touch of something sinister in it, which plays over all Leonardo's work," leads us to another track when he says: [6]

"Besides, the picture is a portrait. From childhood we see this image defining itself on the fabric of his dream; and but for express historical

[6] W. Pater: *The Renaissance*, p. 124, The Macmillan Co., 1910.

A Study in Psychosexuality

testimony, we might fancy that this was but his ideal lady, embodied and beheld at last."

Herzfeld surely must have had something similar in mind when he states that in Mona Lisa Leonardo encountered himself and therefore found it possible to put so much of his own nature into the picture, "whose features from time immemorial have been imbedded with mysterious sympathy in Leonardo's soul."[7]

Let us endeavor to clear up these intimations. It was quite possible that Leonardo was fascinated by the smile of Mona Lisa, because it had awakened something in him which had slumbered in his soul for a long time, in all probability an old memory. This memory was of sufficient importance to stick to him once it had been aroused; he was forced to provide it continually with new expression. The assurance of Pater that we can see an image like that of Mona Lisa defining itself since Leonardo's childhood on the fabric of his dreams seems worthy of belief and deserves to be taken literally.

Vasari mentions as Leonardo's first artistic endeavors, *"teste di femmine che ridono"* ("heads of women who laugh").[8] The passage, which is beyond suspicion, as it is not meant to prove

[7] M. Herzfeld: *Leonardo da Vinci*, p. 88.
[8] Scognamiglio, l.c., p. 32.

anything, reads more precisely as follows: [9] "He formed in his youth some laughing feminine heads out of lime, which have been reproduced in plaster, and some heads of children, which were as beautiful as if modeled by the hands of a master. . . ."

Thus we discover that his practice of art began with the representation of two kinds of objects, which would perforce remind us of the two kinds of sexual objects which we have inferred from the analysis of his vulture phantasy. If the beautiful children's heads were reproductions of his own childish person, then the laughing women were nothing else but reproductions of Caterina, his mother, and we are beginning to have an inkling of the possibility that his mother possessed that mysterious smile which he lost, and which fascinated him so much when he found it again in the Florentine lady.[10]

The painting of Leonardo which in point of time stands nearest to the Mona Lisa is the so-called Saint Anne of the Louvre, representing

[9] L. Schorn, Bd. III, 1843, p. 6.
[10] The same is assumed by Merejkowski, who imagined a childhood for Leonardo which deviates in the essential points from ours, drawn from the results of the vulture phantasy. But if Leonardo himself had displayed this smile, tradition hardly would have failed to report to us this coincidence.

A Study in Psychosexuality

Saint Anne, Mary and the Christ child. It shows the Leonardesque smile most beautifully portrayed in the two feminine heads. It is impossible to find out how much earlier or later than the portrait of Mona Lisa Leonardo began to paint this picture. As both works extended over years, we may well assume that they occupied the master simultaneously. But it would best harmonize with our expectation if his deep interest in the features of Mona Lisa would have instigated Leonardo to form the composition of Saint Anne from his phantasy. For if the smile of Gioconda had conjured up in him the memory of his mother, we would naturally understand that he was first urged to produce a glorification of motherhood, and to give back to her the smile he found in that prominent lady. We may thus allow our interest to glide over from the portrait of Mona Lisa to this other hardly less beautiful picture, now also in the Louvre.

Saint Anne with the daughter and grandchild is a subject seldom treated in the Italian art of painting; at all events Leonardo's representation differs widely from all that is otherwise known. Muther states: [11]

[11] l.c., p. 309.

Leonardo da Vinci

"Some masters like Hans Fries, the older Holbein, and Girolamo dei Libri, made Anne sit near Mary and placed the child between the two. Others like Jakob Corneliscz in his Berlin pictures represented Saint Anne as holding in her arm the small figure of Mary upon which sits the still smaller figure of the Christ child." In Leonardo's picture Mary sits on her mother's lap, bent forward and is stretching out both arms after the boy who plays with a little lamb, and must have slightly maltreated it. The grandmother has one of her unconcealed arms propped on her hip and looks down on both with a blissful smile. The grouping is certainly not quite constrained. But the smile which is playing on the lips of both women, although unmistakably the same as in the picture of Mona Lisa, has lost its sinister and mysterious character; it expresses a calm blissfulness.[12]

On becoming somewhat engrossed in this picture it suddenly dawns upon the spectator that only Leonardo could have painted it, as only he could have formed the vulture phantasy. This picture contains the synthesis of the history of

[12] A. Konstantinowa, l.c., says: "Mary looks tenderly down on her beloved child with a smile that recalls the mysterious expression of la Gioconda." Elsewhere speaking of Mary she says: "The smile of Gioconda floats upon her features."

A Study in Psychosexuality

Leonardo's childhood, the details of which are explainable by the most intimate impressions of his life. In his father's home he found not only the kind stepmother, Donna Albiera, but also the grandmother, his father's mother, Mona Lucia, who, we will assume, was not less tender to him than grandmothers are wont to be. This circumstance must have furnished him with the facts for the representation of a childhood guarded by a mother and grandmother. Another striking feature of the picture assumes still greater significance. Saint Anne, the mother of Mary and the grandmother, who must have been a matron, is formed here perhaps somewhat more mature and more serious than Saint Mary, but still as a young woman of unfaded beauty. As a matter of fact, Leonardo gave the boy two mothers, the one who stretched out her arms after him and another who is seen in the background; both are represented with the blissful smile of maternal happiness. This peculiarity of the picture has not failed to excite the wonder of the authors. Muther, for instance, believes that Leonardo could not bring himself to paint old age, folds and wrinkles, and therefore formed Saint Anne also as a woman of radiant beauty. Whether one can be satisfied with this explana-

Leonardo da Vinci

tion is a question. Other writers have taken occasion to deny generally the sameness of age of mother and daughter.[18] However, Muther's tentative explanation is sufficient proof for the fact that the impression of Saint Anne's youthful appearance was furnished by the picture and is not an imagination produced by a tendency.

Leonardo's childhood was precisely as remarkable as this picture. He has had two mothers, the first his true mother, Caterina, from whom he was torn away between the age of three and five years, and a young tender stepmother, Donna Albiera, his father's wife. By connecting this fact of his childhood with the one mentioned above and condensing them into a uniform fusion, the composition of Saint Anne, Mary and the Child formed itself in him. The maternal form further away from the boy, designated as the grandmother, corresponds in appearance and in spatial relation to the boy, with the real first mother, Caterina. With the blissful smile of Saint Anne, the artist actually disavowed and concealed the envy which the unfortunate mother felt when she was forced to give up her son to her more aristocratic rival, as she had once before her lover.

[18] Cf. v. Seidlitz, l.c., Bd. II, p. 274.

A Study in Psychosexuality

Our feeling that the smile of Mona Lisa del Gioconda awakened in the man the memory of the mother of his first years of childhood would thus be confirmed from another work of Leonardo. Following the production of Mona Lisa, Italian artists depicted in Madonnas and prominent ladies the humble dipping of the head and the peculiar blissful smile of the poor peasant girl, Caterina, who brought to the world the noble son who was destined to paint, investigate and suffer.

When Leonardo succeeded in reproducing in the face of Mona Lisa the double sense comprised in this smile, namely, the promise of unlimited tenderness and sinister threat (in the words of Pater), he remained true even in this to the content of his earliest reminiscence. For the love of the mother became his destiny; it determined his fate and the privations which were in store for him. The impetuosity of the caressing to which the vulture phantasy points was only too natural. The poor forsaken mother had to give vent through mother's love to all her memories of love enjoyed as well as to all her yearnings for more affection; she was forced to it, not only in order to compensate herself for not having a husband, but also the child for not

Leonardo da Vinci

having a father to love it. In the manner of all ungratified mothers she thus took her little son in place of her husband, and robbed him of a part of his virility by maturing too early his erotic life. The love of the mother for the suckling whom she nourishes and cares for is something far deeper-reaching than her later affection for the growing child. It is of the nature of a fully gratified love affair, which fulfills not only all the psychic wishes but also all physical needs, and when it represents one of the forms of happiness attainable by man, it is due, in no little measure, to the possibility of gratifying without reproach also wish feelings which were long repressed and designated as perverse.[14] Even in the happiest young married life the father feels that his child, especially the little boy, has become his rival, and this gives origin to an antagonism against the favorite son which is deeply rooted in the unconscious.

When in the prime of his life Leonardo reencountered that blissful and ecstatic smile as it had once encircled his mother's mouth in caressing, he had long been under the ban of an inhibition, forbidding him ever again to desire such tenderness from women's lips. But as he had

[14] Cf. *Three Contributions to the Theory of Sex* in Freud's *Basic Writings*, l.c.

A Study in Psychosexuality

become a painter he endeavored to reproduce this smile with his brush and furnish all his pictures with it, whether he executed them himself or whether they were done by his pupils under his direction, as in Leda, St. John, and Bacchus. The latter two are variations of the same type. Muther says: "From the locust eater of the Bible Leonardo made a Bacchus, an Apollo, who, with a mysterious smile on his lips, and with his soft thighs crossed, looks on us with infatuated eyes." These pictures breathe a mysticism into the secret of which one dares not penetrate; at most one can make the effort to construct the connection to Leonardo's earlier productions. The figures are again androgynous but no longer in the sense of the vulture phantasy; they are pretty boys of feminine tenderness with feminine forms; they do not cast down their eyes but gaze mysteriously triumphant, as if they knew of a great happy issue concerning which one must remain quiet; the familiar fascinating smile leads us to infer that it is a love secret. It is possible that in these forms Leonardo disavowed and artistically conquered the unhappiness of his love life, in that he represented the wish fulfillment of the boy infatuated with his mother in such blissful union of the male and female nature.

Five

Among the entries in Leonardo's diaries there is one which absorbs the reader's attention through its important content and on account of a small formal error. In July, 1504, he wrote:

"Adi 9 Luglio, 1504, mercoledi, a ore 7 mori Ser Piero da Vinci notalio al palazzo del Potestà, mio padre, a ore 7. Era d'età d'anni 80, lasciò 10 figlioli maschi e 2 feminine." [1]

The notice, as we see, deals with the death of Leonardo's father. The slight error in its form consists in the fact that in the computation of

[1] "On the 9th of July, 1504, Wednesday at 7 o'clock, died Ser Piero da Vinci, notary at the palace of the Podesta, my father, at 7 o'clock. He was eighty years old, left ten sons and two daughters." (E. Müntz, l.c., p. 13.)

A Study in Psychosexuality

the time "at 7 o'clock" is repeated, as if Leonardo had forgotten at the end of the sentence that he had already written it at the beginning. It is only a triviality to which anyone but a psychoanalyst would pay no attention. Perhaps he would not even notice it, or if his attention would be called to it he would say "that can happen to anybody during absent-mindedness or in an affective state and has no other meaning."

The psychoanalyst thinks differently; to him nothing is too trifling as a manifestation of hidden psychic processes; he has long learned that such forgetting or repetition is full of meaning, and that one is indebted to "absent-mindedness" when it makes possible the betrayal of otherwise concealed feelings.

We would say that, like the funeral account of Caterina and the expense account of his pupils, this notice, too, corresponds to a case in which Leonardo was unsuccessful in suppressing his affects, and the long-hidden feeling forcibly obtained a distorted expression. Also the form is similar; it shows the same pedantic precision, the same pushing forward of numbers.[2]

---

[2] I shall overlook a greater error committed by Leonardo in his notice in that he gives his seventy-seven-year-old father eighty years.

Leonardo da Vinci

We call such a repetition a perseveration. It is an excellent means to indicate the affective accentuation. One recalls, for example, Saint Peter's angry speech against his unworthy representative on earth, as given in Dante's *Paradiso:* [3]

"Quegli ch'usurpa in terra il luogo mio
Il luogo mio, il luogo mio, che vaca
Nella presenza del Figliuol di Dio,
Fatto ha del cimiterio mio cloaca."

Without Leonardo's affective inhibition the entry into the diary could perhaps have read as follows: Today at 7 o'clock died my father, Ser Piero da Vinci, my poor father! But the displacement of the perseveration to the most indifferent item of the obituary, to the hour of death, robs the notice of all pathos and lets us recognize that there was something here to conceal and to suppress.

Ser Piero da Vinci, notary and descendant of notaries, was a man of great energy who attained respect and affluence. He was married four times, the two first wives died childless, and not till the

---

[3] "He who usurps on earth my place, my place, my place, which is void in the presence of the Son of God, has made out of my cemetery a sewer." Canto XXXVII.

A Study in Psychosexuality

third marriage had he got the first legitimate son, in 1476, when Leonardo was twenty-four years old, and had long ago changed his father's home for the studio of his master, Verrocchio. With the fourth and last wife whom he married when he was already in the fifties he begot nine sons and two daughters.[4]

To be sure, the father also assumed importance in Leonardo's psychosexual development, and what is more, it was not only in a negative sense, through his absence during the boy's first childhood years, but also directly through his presence in his later childhood. He who as a child desires his mother cannot help wishing to put himself in his father's place, to identify himself with him in his phantasy and later make it his life's task to triumph over him. As Leonardo was not yet five years old when he was received into his paternal home, the young stepmother, Albiera, certainly must have taken the place of his mother in his feeling, and this brought him into that relation of rivalry to his father which may be designated as normal. As is known, the preference for homosexuality did not manifest

[4] It seems that in that passage of the diary Leonardo also erred in the number of his sisters and brothers, which stands in remarkable contrast to its apparent exactness.

Leonardo da Vinci

itself till near the years of puberty. When Leonardo accepted this preference, the identification with the father lost all significance for his sexual life, but continued in other spheres of nonerotic activity. We hear that he was fond of luxury and pretty raiments, and kept servants and horses, although according to Vasari's words, "He hardly possessed anything and worked little." We shall not hold his artistic taste entirely responsible for all these special likings; we recognize in them also the compulsion to copy his father and to excel him. He played the part of the great gentleman to the poor peasant girl; hence the son retained the incentive that he also play the great gentleman; he had the strong feeling "to out-herod Herod," and to show his father exactly how the real high rank looks.

Whoever works as an artist certainly feels as a father to his works. The identification with his father had a fateful result in Leonardo's works of art. He created them and then troubled himself no longer about them, just as his father did not trouble himself about him. The later worriments of his father could change nothing in this compulsion, as the latter originated from the impressions of the first years of childhood, and, the repression having remained uncon-

A Study in Psychosexuality

scious, was incorrigible through later experiences.

At the time of the Renaissance, and even much later, every artist was in need of a gentleman of rank to act as his benefactor. This patron was wont to give the artist commissions for work and entirely controlled his destiny. Leonardo found his patron in Lodovico Sforza, nicknamed Il Moro, a man of high aspirations, ostentatious, diplomatically astute, but of an unstable and unreliable character. In his court in Milan, Leonardo spent the best period of his life, while in his service he evinced his most uninhibited productive activity as is evidenced in The Last Supper, and in the equestrian statue of Francesco Sforza. He left Milan before the catastrophe struck Lodovico Sforza, who died in a French prison. When the news of his benefactor's fate reached Leonardo he made the following entry in his diary: *"Il duca perse lo stato, e la roba, e la libertà, e nessuna sua opera si fini per lui."* ("The duke has lost state, wealth and liberty, not one of his works will be finished by himself.")[5] It is remarkable and surely not without significance that he here raises the same reproach to his benefactor that posterity was to apply to him, as if he wanted to lay the responsibility to a person

[5] v. Seidlitz, l.c., II, p. 270.

who substituted his father-series, for the fact that he himself left his works unfinished. As a matter of fact, he was not wrong in what he said about the duke.

However, if the imitation of his father hurt him as an artist, his resistance against the father was the infantile determinant of his perhaps equally vast accomplishment as an artist. According to Merejkowski's beautiful comparison, he was like a man who awoke too early in the darkness, while the others were all still asleep. He dared utter this bold principle which contains the justification for all independent investigation: *"Chi disputa, allegando l'autorità, non adopra l'ingegno ma piuttosto la memoria."* ("Whoever refers to authorities in disputing ideas, works with his memory rather than with his reason.")[6] Thus he became the first modern natural philosopher, and his courage was rewarded by an abundance of cognitions and anticipations; since the Greek period he was the first to investigate the secrets of nature, relying entirely on his observation and his own judgment. But when he learned to depreciate authority and to reject the imitation of the "ancients" and constantly pointed to the study of nature as

[6] Solmi, *Conferenze Fiorentine*, p. 13.

A Study in Psychosexuality

the source of all wisdom, he only repeated in the highest sublimation attainable to man that which had already obtruded itself on the little boy who surveyed the world with wonder.

To retranslate the scientific abstractions into concrete individual experiences, we would say that the "ancients" and authority only corresponded to the father, and nature again became the tender mother who nourished him. While in most human beings today, as in primitive times, the need for a support of some authority is so imperative that their world becomes shaky when their authority is menaced, Leonardo alone was able to exist without such support; but that would not have been possible had he not been deprived of his father in the first years of his life. The boldness and independence of his later scientific investigation presupposes that his infantile sexual investigation was not inhibited by his father, and this same spirit of scientific independence was continued by his withdrawing from sex.

If anyone like Leonardo escaped in his childhood his father's intimidation and later threw off the shackles of authority in his scientific investigation, it would be in gross contradiction to our expectation if we found that this same man re-

Leonardo da Vinci

mained a believer and was unable to withdraw from dogmatic religion. Psychoanalysis, which has taught us the intimate connection between the father complex and belief in God, has shown us that the personal God is psychologically nothing but an exalted father, and daily demonstrates to us how youthful persons lose their religious belief as soon as the authority of the father breaks down. In the parental complex we thus recognize the roots of religious need; the almighty, just God and kindly nature appear to us as grand sublimations of father and mother, or rather as revivals and restorations of the infantile conceptions of both parents. Religiousness is biologically traced to the long period of helplessness and need of help of the little child. When the child grows up and realizes his loneliness and weakness in the presence of the great forces of life, he then perceives his condition as in childhood and seeks to disavow his despair through a regressive revival of the protecting forces of childhood.[7]

It does not seem that Leonardo's life disproves this conception of religious belief. Accusations charging him with irreligiousness, which in

[7] Cf. *Totem and Taboo* in *The Basic Writings of Sigmund Freud*, l.c.

A Study in Psychosexuality

those times was equivalent to renouncing Christianity, were brought against him already in his lifetime, and were clearly described in the first biography of him by Vasari.[8] In the second edition of his *Vite* (1568) Vasari left out this observation. In view of the extraordinary sensitiveness of his age in matters of religion, it is perfectly comprehensible to us why Leonardo refrained from directly expressing his position to Christianity in his notes. As an investigator he did not permit himself to be misled by the account of the creation of the Holy Scriptures; for instance, he disputed the possibility of a universal flood, and in geology he was as unscrupulous in calculating with hundreds of thousands of years as modern investigators.

Among his "prophecies" one finds some things that would perforce offend the sensitive feelings of a religious Christian, e.g., praying to the images of Saints, reads as follows:[9]

"People talk to people who perceive nothing, who have open eyes and see nothing; they talk to them and receive no answer; they adore those who have ears and hear nothing; they burn lamps for those who do not see."

[8] Müntz, l.c., *La Religion de Léonard*, l.c., p. 292, etc.
[9] Herzfeld, p. 292.

Leonardo da Vinci

Or: Concerning mourning on Good Friday (p. 297):

"In all parts of Europe great peoples will bewail the death of one man who died in the Orient."

It was asserted of Leonardo's art that he took away the last remnant of religious attachment from the holy figures and put them into human form in order to depict in them great and beautiful human feelings. Muther praises him for having overcome the feeling of decadence, and for having returned to man the right of sensuality and pleasurable enjoyment. The entries which show Leonardo absorbed in fathoming the great riddles of nature do not lack any expressions of admiration for the Creator, the last cause of all these wonderful secrets, but nothing indicates that he wished to hold any personal relation to this divine force. The sentences which contain the deep wisdom of his last years breathe the resignation of the man who subjects himself to the 'Ανάγχη, to the laws of nature, and expects no alleviation from the kindness or grace of God. There is hardly any doubt that Leonardo had vanquished dogmatic as well as personal religion, and through his work of investigation

A Study in Psychosexuality

he had withdrawn far from the view of life of the religious Christian.

From our views mentioned before concerning the development of the infantile psychic life, it becomes clear that also Leonardo's first investigations in childhood occupied themselves with the problems of sexuality. But he himself betrays it to us through a transparent veil, in that he connects his impulse to investigate with the vulture phantasy, and in emphasizing the problem of the flight of the bird as one whose elaboration devolved upon him through special concatenations of fate. A very obscure as well as a prophetically sounding passage in his notes dealing with the flight of the bird demonstrates in the nicest way with how much affective interest he clung to the wish that he himself should be able to imitate the art of flying: "The great bird shall take his first flight from the back of his big swan, filling the world with amazement, all writings with his fame, and bring eternal glory to the nest whence he sprang." [10] He probably hoped that he himself would sometimes be able to fly, and we know from the wish-fulfilling dreams of people what

[10] According to M. Herzfeld, L.d.V., p. 32, "Der Grosse Schwan" (the big swan) meant a hill, *Monte Cecero,* near Florence.

bliss one expects from the fulfillment of this hope.

But why do so many people dream of flying? Psychoanalysis answers this question by stating that to fly or to be a bird in the dream is nothing but a concealment of another wish, to the recognition of which we are led by more than one linguistic or real bridge. When the inquisitive child is told that a big bird like the stork brings the little children, when the ancients have formed the phallus winged, when the popular designation of the sexual activity of man is expressed in German by the word "to bird" (vögeln), when the male member is directly called *l'uccello* (bird) by the Italians, all these facts are only small fragments from a large collection which teaches us that the wish to be able to fly signifies in the dream nothing but the longing for the ability of sexual accomplishment. This is an early infantile wish. When the grown-up recalls his childhood, it appears to him as a joyful time, in which one is happy for the moment and looks to the future without any wishes; it is for this reason that he envies children. But the children themselves, if they could inform us about it, would probably give us different reports. It seems that childhood is not that blissful

A Study in Psychosexuality

idyl into which we later distort it, that, on the contrary, children are lashed through the years of childhood by the wish to become big, and to imitate the grown-ups. This wish instigates all their playing. If in the course of their sexual investigation children feel that the grown-up knows something wonderful concerning the mysterious and yet so important realm that they are prohibited from knowing or doing, they are seized with a violent wish to know it, and dream of it in the form of flying, or prepare this disguise of the wish for their later flying dreams. Thus aviation, which has attained its aim in our times, has also its infantile erotic roots.

By admitting that he entertained a special personal relation to the problem of flying since his childhood, Leonardo confirms what we must assume from the investigation of children of our own times, namely, that his childhood investigation was directed to sexual matters. At least this one problem escaped the repression which later estranged him from sexuality. From childhood until the age of perfect intellectual maturity this subject, slightly varied, continued to hold his interest, and it is quite possible that he was as little successful in the attainment of his cherished art in the primary sexual sense as in the

Leonardo da Vinci

mechanical, that both wishes were denied to him.

As a matter of fact, the great Leonardo remained infantile in some ways throughout his whole life; it is said that all great men must retain something of the infantile. As a grown-up he still continued playing, which sometimes made him appear strange and incomprehensible to his contemporaries. When he constructed the most artistic mechanical toys for court festivities and receptions, we were displeased by it, because we disliked to see the master waste his power on such petty stuff. He himself did not seem averse to giving his time to such things. Vasari reports that he did similar things even when not urged to it by request: "There (in Rome) he made a doughy mass out of wax, and when it softened he formed thereof very delicate animals filled with air; when he blew into them they flew in the air, and when the air was exhausted they fell to the ground. For a peculiar lizard caught by the wine-dresser of Belvedere, Leonardo made wings from skin pulled off from other lizards, which he filled with mercury so that they moved and trembled when it walked; he then made for it eyes, a beard and horns, tamed it and put it in a little box and

A Study in Psychosexuality

terrified all his friends with it." [11] Such playing often served him as an expression of serious thoughts: "He had often cleaned the intestines of a sheep so well that one could hold them in the hollow of the hand; he then brought them into a big room, and attached them to a blacksmith's bellows which he kept in an adjacent room; he then blew them up until they filled up the whole room so that everybody had to crowd into a corner. In this manner he showed how they gradually became transparent and filled with air, and as they were at first confined to very small space and gradually became bigger and bigger in the large room, he compared the whole process to a genius." [12] His fables and riddles evince the same playful pleasure in harmless concealment and artistic masking; the riddles were put into the form of prophecies; almost all are rich in ideas and to a remarkable degree devoid of wit.

The plays and leaps which Leonardo allowed his phantasy have in some cases quite misled his biographers who misunderstood this part of his nature. In Leonardo's Milanese manuscripts one

[11] Vasari, translated by Schorn, 1843.
[12] Ebenda, p. 39.

Leonardo da Vinci

finds, for example, outlines of letters to the "Diodario of Sorio (Syria), Viceroy of the holy Sultan of Babylon," in which Leonardo presents himself as an engineer sent to these regions of the Orient in order to construct some works. In these letters he defends himself against the reproach of laziness; he furnishes geographical descriptions of cities and mountains; and finally he discusses a big elementary event which occurred while he was there.[13]

In 1881, J. P. Richter endeavored to prove from these documents that Leonardo made these traveler's observations when he really was in the service of the Sultan of Egypt, and that while in the Orient he embraced the Mohammedan religion. This sojourn in the Orient should have taken place in the time of 1483, that is, before he removed to the court of the Duke of Milan. However, it was not difficult for other authors to recognize the illustrations of this supposed journey to the Orient for what they really were, namely, fantastic productions of the youthful artist which he created for his own amusement, and in which he probably brought to expression

[13] Concerning these letters and the combinations connected with them see Müntz, l.c., p. 82; for the wording of the same and for the notices connected with them see Herzfeld, l.c., p. 223.

A Study in Psychosexuality

his wishes to see the world and experience adventures.

A fantastic formation is probably also the "Academia Vinciana," the acceptance of which is based on the existence of five or six very artistic and intricate emblems with the inscription of the Academy. Vasari mentions these drawings but not the Academy.[14] Müntz who placed such ornament on the cover of his big work on Leonardo belongs to the few who believe in the reality of an "Academia Vinciana."

It is probable that this impulse to play disappeared in Leonardo's maturer years, that it became dissipated in his investigating activity which constituted the last and highest development of his personality. But the fact that it continued so long may teach us how slowly one tears himself away from his infantilism after having enjoyed in his childhood a supreme erotic happiness, which is later unattainable.

[14] Besides, he lost some time in that he even made a drawing of a braided cord in which one could follow the thread from one end to the other, until it formed a perfectly circular figure; a very difficult and beautiful drawing of this kind is engraved on copper; in the center of it one can read the words: "Leonardus Vinci Academia" (p. 8).

Six

It would be futile to disregard the fact that, at present, readers in general find every pathography unsavory. This attitude is cloaked with the reproach that from a pathographic elaboration of a great man one never obtains an understanding of his importance and his attainments, that it is therefore useless mischief to study in him things which could just as well be found in every Tom, Dick and Harry. However, this criticism is so clearly unjust that it can only be understandable when viewed as a pretext and a disguise for something else. As a matter of fact, the aim of a pathography is not to make comprehensible the attainments of the great man; one should really not be blamed for not doing

A Study in Psychosexuality

something which he never promised. The real motives for the opposition are quite different. One finds them when one bears in mind that biographers are fixated on their heroes in a very peculiar manner. They frequently select the hero as the object of study because, for personal reasons of their own emotional life, they had a special affection for him from the very outset. They then devote themselves to a work of idealization, which strives to enroll the great man among their infantile models, and to revive through him, as it were, their infantile conception of the father. For the sake of this wish they wipe out the individual features in his physiognomy, they rub out the traces of his life's struggle with inner and outer resistances, and do not tolerate in him anything savoring of human weakness or imperfection; they then give us a cold, strange, ideal form instead of a man to whom we could feel distantly related. It is to be regretted that they do this, for they thereby sacrifice the truth to an illusion, and for the sake of their infantile phantasies they let slip the opportunity to penetrate into the most attractive secrets of human nature.[1]

[1] This criticism holds quite generally and is not aimed at Leonardo's biographers in particular.

Leonardo da Vinci

Leonardo himself, judging from his love for the truth and his inquisitiveness, would have interposed no objections to our effort of discovering the determinations of his psychic and intellectual development from the trivial peculiarities and riddles of his nature. We respect him by learning from him. It does no injury to his greatness to study the sacrifices which his development from the child must have entailed, and to compile the factors which have stamped on his person the tragic feature of failure.

Let us expressly emphasize that we have never considered Leonardo as a neurotic or as a "nervous person" in the sense of this awkward term. Whoever takes it amiss that we should even dare apply to him viewpoints gained from pathology still clings to prejudices which we have now justly given up. We no longer believe that health and disease, normal and nervous, are sharply distinguished from each other, and that neurotic traits must be considered as proofs of a general inferiority. We know today that neurotic symptoms are substitutive formations for certain repressive acts, which must result in the course of our development from the child to the cultural man, that we all produce such substitutive formations, and that only the amount,

A Study in Psychosexuality

intensity and distribution of these substitutive formations justify the practical conception of illness and the conclusion of constitutional inferiority. According to the slight indications in Leonardo's personality we would place him near that neurotic type which we designate as the "obsessive type," and we would compare his investigations with the "reasoning mania" of neurotics, and his inhibitions with the so-called "abulias" of the same.

The object of our work was to explain the inhibitions in Leonardo's sexual life and in his artistic activity. For this purpose we shall now sum up what we could discover concerning the course of his psychic development.

We were unable to gain any knowledge about his hereditary factors; on the other hand, we recognize that the accidental circumstances of his childhood produced a far-reaching disturbing effect. His illegitimate birth deprived him of the influence of a father until perhaps his fifth year, and left him to the tender seduction of a mother whose only consolation he was. Having been kissed by her into sexual prematurity, he surely must have entered into a phase of infantile sexual activity of which only one single manifestation is definitely shown: namely, the

Leonardo da Vinci

intensity of his infantile sexual investigation. The impulse for looking and inquisitiveness were most strongly stimulated by his impressions from early childhood; the erogenous oral-zone received an accentuation which it had never given up. From his later contrasting behavior, such as his exaggerated sympathy for animals, we can conclude that this infantile period did not lack strong sadistic traits.

An energetic shift of repression put an end to this infantile excess and established the dispositions which became manifest in the years of puberty. The most striking result of this transformation was a turning away from all gross sensual activities. Leonardo was able to lead a life of abstinence and thus gave the impression of an asexual person. When the boy was deluged by the floods of pubescent excitement they did not make him ill by forcing him to costly and harmful substitutive formations; thanks to his early preference for sexual inquisitiveness, the greater part of his sexual needs could be sublimated into a general thirst for knowledge and thus evade repression. A much smaller portion of the libido was turned to sexual aims, and represented the stunted sexual life of the grown-up. In consequence of the repression of the love for

A Study in Psychosexuality

the mother, this portion assumed a homosexual attitude and manifested itself as ideal love for boys. The fixation on the mother, as well as the happy reminiscences of his relations with her, were preserved in his unconscious but remained for the time in an inactive state. In this manner were repression, fixation and sublimation distributed in the disposal of the contributions which the sexual impulse furnished to Leonardo's psychic life.

From the obscure age of boyhood Leonardo appears to us as an artist, a painter and sculptor, thanks to a specific talent which was probably enforced in the first years of childhood by the early awakening of his impulse for looking. We would gladly report in what way his artistic activity depends on the primal forces of his psyche, if our material had not here proved inadequate. We content ourselves by emphasizing the fact, concerning which there is now hardly any doubt, that the productions of the artist also give an outlet to his sexual desire. In the case of Leonardo we can refer to the information imparted by Vasari that heads of laughing women and pretty boys, that is, representations of his sexual objects, attracted attention among his first artistic efforts. It seems that during his flourish

Leonardo da Vinci

ing youth Leonardo at first worked in an uninhibited manner. As he took his father as a model for his outer conduct in life, he passed through a period of manly creative power and artistic productivity in Milan, where favored by fate he found a substitute for his father in Duke Lodovico Sforza. But our experience, that an almost complete suppression of the real sexual life does not furnish the most favorable conditions for the activity of sublimated sexual strivings, was soon confirmed in him. The first form of his sexual life asserted itself; his activity and ability to quick decisions began to weaken; the tendency to reflection and delay was already noticeable as a disturbance in The Last Supper; and this influence on his technique determined the fate of this magnificent work. Slowly a process developed in him which can be put parallel only to the regressions of neurotics. His development at puberty into the artist was outstripped by the early infantile determinant of the investigator; the second sublimation of his erotic impulses receded in the face of the very first ones which were prepared during the first repression. He became an investigator, first in the service of his art, later independently and away from his art. With the loss of his patron,

A Study in Psychosexuality

the substitute for his father, and with the increasing difficulties in his life, the regressive supplement continually increased. He became *"impacientissimo al pennello"* ("most impatient with the brush") as reported by a correspondent of Countess Isabella d'Este who desired to possess at any cost a painting from his hand.[2] His infantile past had gained control over him. The investigation, however, which now took the place of his artistic production, seems to have borne certain traits which betrayed the activity of unconscious impulses; this was seen in his insatiability, his regardless obstinacy, and in his lack of ability to adjust himself to actual conditions.

At the zenith of his life, at the age of the first fifties, at a time when the sex characteristics of women have already undergone a regressive change, and when the libido in men not infrequently ventures into an energetic rise, a new transformation came over him. Still deeper strata of his psychic content became active again, but this further regression was of benefit to his art, which was in a state of deterioration. He met the woman who awakened in him the memory of the happy and sensuously enraptured smile of his

[2] Seidlitz, II, p. 271.

Leonardo da Vinci

mother, and under the influence of this awakening he reacquired the stimulus which guided him in the beginning of his artistic efforts when he formed the smiling women. He then painted Mona Lisa, Saint Anne, and a number of mystic pictures which were all characterized by the enigmatic smile. With the help of his oldest erotic feelings he triumphed in conquering once more the inhibition in his art. This last development faded away in the obscurity of his advancing age. But even before this his intellect rose to the highest capacity of a philosophy of life which was far ahead of his time.

In the preceding chapters I have shown what justification one may have for such delineation of Leonardo's course of development, for this manner of linking his life and for explaining his wavering between art and science. If after these explanations I should evoke the criticism from even friends and adepts of psychoanalysis, that I have only written a psychoanalytic romance, I should answer that I certainly did not overestimate the reliability of these results. Like others, I succumbed to the attraction which emanated from this great and mysterious man, in whose being one seems to sense forceful and impelling

A Study in Psychosexuality

passions, which nevertheless evince themselves in a remarkably subdued manner.

But whatever may be the truth about Leonardo's life we cannot relinquish our effort to investigate it psychoanalytically before we have finished another task. In general, we must fix the limits of what psychoanalysis can accomplish in biography in order that every omitted explanation should not be held up to us as a failure. Psychoanalytic investigation has at its disposal the data of the history of the person's life, which, on the one hand, consist of accidental events and environmental influences, and, on the other hand, of the reported reactions of the individual. Based on the knowledge of psychic mechanisms, psychoanalysis then seeks to investigate dynamically the character of the individual from his reactions, and to lay bare his earliest psychic motive forces as well as their later transformations and developments. If this succeeds, then the behavior of the personality is explained through the co-operation of constitutional and accidental factors, or through inner and outer forces. If such an undertaking, as perhaps in the case of Leonardo, does not yield definite results, then the blame for it is not to be laid to the

Leonardo da Vinci

faulty or inadequate psychoanalytic method, but to the vague and fragmentary material left by tradition about this person. It is, therefore, only the author, who forced psychoanalysis to furnish an expert opinion on such insufficient material, who is responsible for the failure.

However, even if one had at his disposal very rich historical material and could make the best use of the psychic mechanisms, a psychoanalytic investigation of two important questions could not possibly furnish a definite view that the individual would turn out only so and not differently. Concerning Leonardo we had to take the view that the accident of his illegitimate birth and the pampering of his mother exerted the most decisive influence on his character formation, and on his later fate, through the fact that the sexual repression following this infantile phase caused him to sublimate his libido into a thirst for knowledge, which conditioned his sexual inactivity for his entire later life. The repression, however, which followed the first erotic gratification of childhood did not have to take place; in another individual it would perhaps not have taken place, or it would have turned out not nearly as profuse. We must recognize here a degree of freedom which can no

A Study in Psychosexuality

longer be solved psychoanalytically. One is as little justified in representing the issue of this shift of repression as the only one possible. It is quite probable that another person would not have succeeded in withdrawing the main part of his libido from the repression and then sublimating it into a desire for knowledge; under the same influences as Leonardo, another person might have sustained a permanent injury to his intellectual work, or an uncontrollable disposition to compulsion neurosis. The two characteristics of Leonardo also make it impossible for psychoanalytic investigation to explain, first, his particular tendency to repress his impulses, and, second, his extraordinary ability to sublimate the primitive impulses.

The impulses and their transformations are the last things psychoanalysis can discern. Henceforth it leaves the stage to biological investigation. The tendency to repression, as well as the ability to sublimate, must be traced back to the organic bases of the character, upon which alone the psychic structure arises. As artistic talent and productive ability are intimately connected with sublimation, we have to admit also that the nature of artistic attainment is psychoanalytically inaccessible to us. Biological investigation

Leonardo da Vinci

of our time endeavors to explain the chief traits of the organic constitution of a person through the fusion of male and female predispositions in the material sense; Leonardo's physical beauty as well as his left-handedness furnish here some support. However, we do not wish to leave the ground of pure psychological investigation. Our aim remains to demonstrate the connection between outer experiences and reactions of the person over the path of the instinctual activity. Even if psychoanalysis does not explain to us the fact of Leonardo's artistic accomplishment, it still gives us an understanding of its expressions and limitations. It does seem, however, as if only a man with Leonardo's childhood experiences could have painted Mona Lisa and Saint Anne, and could have prepared that sad fate for his works and so attain unheard-of fame as a naturalist; it seems as if the key to all his attainments and failures was hidden in the childhood phantasy of the vulture.

But may not one take offense at the results of an investigation which concede to the accidents of parental constellation so decisive an influence on the fate of a person, which, for example, subordinates Leonardo's fate to his illegitimate

A Study in Psychosexuality

birth and to the sterility of his first stepmother, Donna Albiera? I believe that one has no right to feel so; if one considers accident as unworthy of determining our fate, one only relapses to the pious philosophy of life, the overcoming of which Leonardo himself prepared when he put down in writing that the sun does not move. We are naturally grieved over the fact that a just God and a kindly providence do not guard us better against such influences in our most defenseless age. We thereby easily forget that, as a matter of fact, everything in our life is accident, from our very origin through the meeting of the spermatozoon and ovum, an accident, which nevertheless participates in the lawfulness and fatalities of nature, lacking only the connection to our wishes and illusions. The division of life's determinants into the "fatalities" of our constitution and the "accidents" of our childhood may still be indefinite in individual cases, but taken altogether one can no longer entertain any doubt about the precise importance of our first years of childhood. We all still show too little respect for nature, which, in Leonardo's deep words recalling Hamlet's speech, *"is full of infinite reasons which never appeared in experi-*

ence." [3] Every one of us human beings corresponds to one of the infinite experiments in which these "reasons of nature" force themselves into experience.

[3] "*La natura e piena d'infinite ragione che non furono mai in isperienza,*" M. Herzfeld, l.c., p. 11.